Multiple Choice Questions in Anaesthesiology

Ann E. Black
Consultant Anaesthetist
Great Ormond Street Hospital for Children
London WC1N 3JH

Andrea A. Kelleher
Consultant Anaesthetist
Royal Brompton Hospital
London SW3 6NP

Catherine A. Shaw
Consultant Anaesthetist
Whittington Hospital
Highgate Hill, London N19 5NF

SECOND EDITION

 PETROC PRESS

Petroc Press, an imprint of LibraPharm Limited

Distributors
Plymbridge Distributors Limited, Plymbridge House, Estover Road, Plymouth PL6 7PZ, UK

First edition published 1994 by Kluwer Academic Publishers
Second edition published 2003 © LibraPharm Limited

Published in the United Kingdom by
◆ LibraPharm Limited
Gemini House
162 Craven Road
Newbury
Berkshire
RG14 5NR
UK

A catalogue record for this book is available from the British Library

ISBN 1 900603 09 8

Typeset by WordSpace, Lewes, East Sussex

Printed and bound in the United Kingdom by
MPG Books Limited, Bodmin, Cornwall PL31 1EG

Multiple Choice Questions in Anaesthesiology

WITHDRAWN

Other Examination Preparation Books Published by Petroc Press:

Obtainable from all good booksellers or, in case of difficulty, from Plymbridge Distributors Limited, Plymbridge House, Estover Road, Plymouth, Devon PL6 7PZ; Tel: 01752 202300, Fax: 01752 202333.

Contents

Foreword to the Second Edition

The examinations for the Fellowship of The Royal College of Anaesthetists (FRCA) are tough, but fair. They play a major role in maintaining standards of anaesthesia in the UK. Candidates are well aware that passing the multiple choice paper of the final FRCA examination is an essential first step in the process. As an examiner, I know that a 'good' pass enhances a candidate's chances of ultimate success in the overall scheme of the examination.

This excellent book, *Multiple Choice Questions in Anaesthesiology*, has been compiled by three practising consultant anaesthetists to prepare the final FRCA candidate for the minefield of the multiple choice paper. It provides a comprehensive overview of the type of questions that a candidate will be expected to answer, and, aided by the detailed explanations, will in addition remind the candidate of any areas of revision he or she has not covered.

Lack of basic knowledge, not surprisingly, is the most significant reason for examination failure. This book will help the final FRCA candidate to recognise and circumvent this problem.

John W. W. Gothard, MB BS FFARCS DObst RCOG
Consultant Anaesthetist, the Brompton Hospital, London
October 2002

1. Anaesthesia and Intensive Care

Q1.1 Venous air embolism may be characterised by:

A. a tachycardia
B. a machinery murmur on auscultation of the precordium
C. reduction in both end tidal carbon dioxide and arterial oxygen tension
D. ventricular fibrillation
E. bronchospasm

Q1.2 A 5-year-old child presents with bleeding 5 hours following adenotonsillectomy. He has a heart rate of 160/min, cool peripheries, and is coughing up blood. Acceptable management includes:

A. immediate transfer to the operating theatre
B. induction of anaesthesia on the ward as an emergency in order to secure the airway
C. when intubated, a size 4.5 or 5.0 mm endotracheal tube is appropriate
D. rapid sequence induction with cricoid pressure must be used
E. the avoidance of an orogastric tube for fear of restarting the haemorrhage

Q1.3 Postoperative urinary retention may be associated with:

A. raised intracranial pressure
B. perineal surgery
C. neostigmine administration
D. hypotension
E. diabetes mellitus

Q1.4 When anaesthetising a patient for laser surgery of the airway:

A. the cuffed endotracheal tube may be safely inflated with air
B. an inspired oxygen fraction of 1.0 is usually required
C. techniques using jet ventilation have an increased incidence of awareness
D. jet ventilation is safe in the obstructed airway
E. transtracheal ventilation may be necessary

Q1.5 On a standard posteroanterior radiograph of the chest:

A. the cardiothoracic ratio increases with age
B. a pneumothorax will increase in size on inspiration
C. an indistinct right heart border suggests pathology in the right lower lobe
D. the azygos lobe is seen in the right upper zone
E. the right hilum is usually one to two centimetres higher that the left

Q1.6 When considering general anaesthesia for dental surgery:

A. it may be safely given in general dental practice
B. patients are usually fit for discharge within 30 minutes
C. trismus associated with a dental abscess usually relaxes with general anaesthesia
D. preoperative investigations are not necessary
E. cardiac arrhythmias are uncommon

Q1.7 A 74-year-old man who has undergone hemicolectomy 12 hours previously is found to have a blood pressure of 70/40, temperature of 37.3°C, respiratory rate of 24 breaths/min, arterial oxygen saturation 92% in air, CVP 14 mm Hg, PCWP 22 mm Hg and a cardiac index of 2.2 litres min^{-1} m^{-2}. His initial management should include:

A. immediate intubation and ventilation
B. intravenous antibiotics
C. the intravenous infusion of 500ml of colloid
D. urinary catheterisation
E. inotropic support

Q1.8 Regarding awake tracheal intubation:

A. atropine premedication is essential
B. cocaine is the agent of choice to provide anaesthesia of the nasal passages
C. nebulised 4% lignocaine may be used as the sole anaesthetic agent
D. indications may include patients with a 'full stomach'
E. fibreoptic laryngoscopy is not required

Q1.9 The management of acute respiratory distress syndrome (ARDS) may include:

A. reversal of the I:E ratio
B. being nursed in the prone position
C. steroids
D. nitrous oxide
E. permissive hypocapnia

Q1.10 Prophylactic antibiotics prior to dental treatment are not required for patients with the following conditions:

A. untreated secundum atrial septal defect
B. one year following trans-catheter device closure of the secundum atrial septal defect
C. one year following cardiac surgery to close the secundum atrial septal defect
D. following surgical ligation of a patent ductus arteriosus
E. a child with an innocent cardiac murmur

Q1.11 When anaesthetising a patient for the surgical management of a fractured mandible:

A. preoxygenation may prove difficult
B. wire cutters may be necessary postoperatively
C. conventional laryngoscopy and intubation are rarely possible
D. nasal endotracheal intubation is necessary
E. the postoperative management is routinely carried out in HDU/ITU

Q1.12 Septic shock:

A. is always caused by Gram-negative organisms
B. may be associated with a decrease in cardiac index
C. is associated with an increase in circulating interleukin-2 and tumour necrosis factor
D. may be complicated by disseminated intravascular coagulation
E. the probability of survival is proportional to the serum lactate concentration

Q1.13 The following statements are true of acute spinal cord injury:

A   it most commonly occurs in the thoracic region
B   spinal shock is characterised by muscle rigidity and increased blood pressure
C   pulmonary oedema is often a complication of acute cervical cord injury
D   tracheal intubation is indicated if the vital capacity falls below 20 ml kg^{-1}
E   fibreoptic intubation is always indicated in the presence of an unstable cervical spine

Q1.14 In the anaesthetic management of phaeochromocytoma:

A.   preoperative alpha blockade with phenylephrine is mandatory
B.   preoperative beta blockade must be established prior to the institution of an alpha blocker
C.   pancuronium is the relaxant of choice
D.   hypoglycaemia is a common postoperative complication
E.   due to recently improved survival following resection of this tumour, invasive arterial monitoring is no longer required for surgery

Q1.15 When considering a tracheal tube for a normal child:

A.   a 5.5 mm tracheal tube is likely to be suitable for a child aged 2 years
B.   the length of a tracheal tube is approximately twice the outer diameter of the tube
C.   the size chosen is approximately the same as the diameter of the child's little finger
D.   cuffed tubes are never used in children under 8 years
E.   the nasal route is avoided between 3 and 6 years because of the presence of adenoidal tissue

Q1.16 In a child who is ASA 1 or 2:

A.   routine surgery should always be cancelled in a child with an upper respiratory tract infection (URTI)
B.   the greatest risk of airway complications occurs with a recent URTI
C.   following confirmed accidental aspiration of gastric contents, chest signs are always present
D.   a preoperative haemoglobin is helpful in all children under 3 years
E.   the sickledex test may be negative in babies less than three months who will have sickle cell disease

Q1.17 A high central venous pressure in the presence of circulatory failure occurs in:

A. cardiac failure
B. haemorrhage
C. tension pneumothorax
D. pulmonary embolism
E. air embolism

Q1.18 When compared to adults, neonates have:

A. a lower oxygen consumption relative to their size
B. an anterior larynx which is narrowest at the level of the cricoid
C. an estimated blood volume of 75 ml kg^{-1}
D. a tendency to become hypoglycaemic if the preoperative fast is prolonged
E. a well developed shivering response to hypothermia

Q1.19 In patients who have had organ transplantation:

A. sudden death following heart transplant can occur due to atherosclerosis
B. early failure of the transplanted kidney may be associated with venous thrombosis
C. survival post heart transplant is approximately 20% at five years
D. endogenous catecholamines are ineffective following heart transplantation
E. patients having bone marrow transplants should receive irradiated blood products

Q1.20 A subclavian perivascular block of the brachial plexus may be complicated by:

A. hoarse voice
B. intra-arterial injection of the local anaesthetic
C. a Horner syndrome
D. phrenic nerve palsy
E. intrathecal injection of local anaesthetic

Q1.21 Reflex sympathetic dystrophy:

A. can be treated with local guanethidine block
B. may occur after minor trauma
C. is associated with changes on bone scan which are diagnostic
D. does not occur in children
E. responds well to short courses of opiates

Q1.22 Pain can be decreased by:

A. inhibition at NMDA receptors
B. excitation at GABA receptors
C. dorsal column stimulation
D. behavioural modification
E. opiate activity at the μ_2-receptor

Q1.23 Complications related to pain relief strategies include:

A. morphine metabolites affect platelet function
B. fentanyl has a more rapid onset than morphine when given intrathecally, but is shorter-lasting
C. longterm use of non-steroidal anti-inflammatory agents is associated with delayed gastric emptying
D. non-steroidal anti-inflammatory agents affect platelet function by causing platelet aggregation
E. pethidine metabolites accumulate in patients with renal failure

Q1.24 A brachial plexus block via the axilla using 0.25% bupivacaine:

A. is contraindicated if the axillary artery has been transfixed
B. is unlikely to last longer than 3 hours
C. is associated with permanent damage of the brachial plexus
D. is contraindicated in children
E. may be complicated by a phrenic nerve palsy

Q1.25 In the management of chronic pain:

A. a coeliac plexus block with phenol is effective in pancreatic pain
B. transcutaneous nerve stimulation is the best treatment for trigeminal neuralgia
C. epidural steroids may be associated with chronic arachnoiditis
D. antiepileptic medication is useful in trigeminal neuralgia
E. antidepressant medication may be useful

Q1.26 Complications of a stellate ganglion block include:

A. pupillary constriction
B. ptosis
C. hyperhidrosis of the ipsilateral face
D. a warm upper limb
E. nasal congestion

Q1.27 Sympathetic blockade may be useful in the management of:

A. reflex sympathetic dystrophy
B. peripheral vascular disease
C. inadvertent intra-arterial injection of thiopentone
D. hyperhidrosis
E. diabetic neuropathy

Q1.28 Prolonged exposure to nitrous oxide may result in:

A. reduced methionine synthetase activity
B. increased sensitivity to non-depolarising muscle relaxants
C. reduced numbers of circulating platelets
D. megaloblastic bone marrow changes
E. peripheral neuropathy

Q1.29 Factors predisposing to Acute Respiratory Distress Syndrome following trauma include:

A. aspiration
B. multiple fractures
C. pulmonary contusion
D. the requirement of a blood transfusion greater than 12 units
E. a systolic blood pressure of less than 90mmHg for more than 30 minutes

Q1.30 The Trauma Score is used to assess status in triage and includes scores for:

A. respiratory rate
B. heart rate
C. mean blood pressure
D. Glasgow Coma Score
E. the number of long bone fractures

Q1.31 When providing regional anaesthesia for ophthalmic surgery:

A. larger volumes of local anaesthetic are required for a retrobulbar block than a peribulbar block
B. retrobulbar haemorrhage is more common when a retrobulbar block is performed than with the peribulbar approach
C. perforation of the globe is more common if the axial length is less than 2.6 cm
D. tachycardia is common
E. facial nerve block is necessary to supplement peribulbar block in order to achieve surgical anaesthesia

Q1.32 Infections known to be transmitted from donor to recipient by blood transfusion include:

A. cytomegalovirus
B. hepatitis A
C. malaria
D. variant CJD
E. syphilis

Q1.33 Reported complications of transoesophageal echocardiography include:

A. oesophageal rupture
B. hoarse voice
C. cardiac arrhythmias
D. bronchospasm
E. predisposition to subsequent pharyngeal pouch formation

Q1.34 Successful intubation of the trachea may reliably be confirmed by:

A. a posterior–anterior chest x-ray
B. the presence of bilateral breath sounds
C. fibreoptic bronchoscopy
D. the presence of moisture within the endotracheal tube
E. an end tidal carbon dioxide measurement of 8.5 kPa

Q1.35 The following interventions may be used to reduce intracranial pressure:

A. hypoventilation
B. intravenous dexamethasone
C. the application of PEEP
D. thiopentone infusion
E. intravenous frusemide

Q1.36 Adequate preoxygenation may be achieved by:

A. 4 vital capacity breaths of 100% oxygen
B. 3 minutes of normal tidal ventilation with 100% oxygen
C. 3 vital capacity breaths of 100% oxygen
D. 5 minutes of normal tidal ventilation breathing 50% oxygen
E. 6 vital capacity breaths with 50% oxygen

Q1.37 The following statements are true of malignant hyperpyrexia:

A. one of the genes responsible has been located on the long arm of chromosome 19
B. the temperature rises at a maximum rate of 2°C/hr
C. it should be suspected if there is an unexplained decrease in end tidal carbon dioxide concentration
D. dantrolene should be given in an initial dose of 1 mg kg^{-1}
E. masseter spasm may be an early sign

Q1.38 According to the Resuscitation Council (UK) Guidelines (2000), the management of ventricular fibrillation (VF) in an adult may include:

A. up to 3 synchronised DC shocks with energies of 200J, 200J, 360J given as immediate management
B. external cardiac massage at a rate of 100 compressions per minute without interruption for ventilation
C. adrenaline 1 mg kg⁻¹ every 3 minutes
D. amiodarone 300 mg may be given via a peripheral vein to treat refractory VF
E. an anterior–posterior position of the paddles is associated with an increased chance of successful defibrillation

Q1.39 During anaesthesia in a patient with a permanent pacemaker the following statements are true:

A. bipolar diathermy may be used
B. during diathermy a burn may occur at the tip of the pacemaker wire, raising the threshold and resulting in pacemaker failure
C. pacemaker dependence should be determined preoperatively
D. adrenaline is the drug of choice if pacemaker failure occurs
E. the serum potassium level should be checked preoperatively

Q1.40 Intraocular pressure may be increased by:

A. nitrous oxide
B. suxamethonium
C. mannitol
D. hypercapnoea
E. hypoxia

Q1.41 Indications for a preoperative chest x-ray include:

A. age over 60 years
B. cigarette smoking
C. recent immigration from an area where TB is endemic unless recent films are available
D. possible evidence of metastasis
E. established cardiorespiratory disease in patients who have not had a chest x-ray within the last 12 months

Q1.42 Absolute indications for the placement of a double-lumen endobroncheal tube include:

A. massive haematemesis
B. bronchopleural fistula
C. right lower lobectomy
D. giant lung cyst
E. oesophagectomy

Q1.43 The diagnosis of brain stem death in the United Kingdom requires:

A. core temperature greater than 35°C
B. no EEG activity
C. absence of all sedative and muscle relaxant drugs
D. no limb movements
E. a loss of the doll's eye reflex

Q1.44 A 20-year-old male is admitted following a motorcycle accident having sustained bilateral fractured femurs. The following findings may cause you to suspect fat embolism:

A. pulmonary oedema
B. thrombocytopenia
C. hypocalcaemia
D. confusion
E. fat droplets in the urine

Q1.45 The following statements are true of intraoperative cell salvage:

A. it is indicated when the anticipated blood loss is greater than 20% of the patient's estimated blood volume
B. it is not feasible in children less than 30 kg because of the small volume of blood salvaged
C. the salvaged red blood cells are suspended in citrate-phosphate-dextrose additive solution
D. it may be acceptable to patients with religious objections to blood transfusion
E. it may be complicated by hepatic impairment if the cells are inadequately washed.

Q1.46 The following statements are true of intravenous fluids:

A. 1 litre of 5% dextrose contains 50 mg of glucose
B. Hartmann's solution contains 29 mmol of lactate per litre
C. hydroxyethyl starch has a mean molecular weight of 35,000 daltons
D. normal saline solution contains 70 mmol of sodium per litre
E. Hartmann's solution contains 5 mmol of phosphate per litre

Q1.47 Oxygen therapy is indicated in the following:

A. carbon monoxide poisoning
B. cardiac tamponade
C. major haemorrhage
D. thyrotoxic crisis
E. pneumothorax

Q1.48 The following features may lead you to suspect a total spinal during attempted epidural anaesthesia:

A. severe hypotension
B. widely dilated pupils indicative of cerebral damage
C. rapid onset of symptoms
D. hyperventilation
E. recovery within two hours

Q1.49 The following features may be predictive of a difficult intubation:

A. increased atlanto–occipital distance
B. decreased posterior mandibular depth
C. Mallampati grade III
D. A Wilson score of less than 2
E. A thyromental distance less than 6 cms

Q1.50 The following features are consistent with a diagnosis of amniotic fluid embolism:

A. pre-existing pregnancy-induced hypertension
B. haemoptysis
C. precipitous labour
D. disseminated intravascular coagulation
E. aspiration of amniotic debris from a central venous catheter

Q1.51 Obstructive sleep apnoea is associated with:

A. systemic hypertension
B. pulmonary hypertension
C. tonsillar hypertrophy
D. hypothyroidism
E. Ondine's curse

Q1.52 Effective cricoid pressure is dependent upon:

A. an intact cricoid cartilage
B. preoxygenation
C. aspiration of the nasogastric tube prior to induction
D. occlusion of the lumen of the oesophagus by compressing it against the body of the sixth cervical vertebra
E. the application of a force of at least 40 N

Q1.53 A 22-year-old male was admitted following a car accident with a ruptured spleen and lacerated liver. During resuscitation he received 15 units of packed red blood cells. This management may be complicated by:

A. hypercalcaemia
B. hyperkalaemia
C. persistent bleeding
D. alkalosis
E. idiopathic thrombocytopaenia

Q1.54 The following features are associated with ageing:

A. a 15% reduction in functional residual capacity at age 80 years
B. a 20% reduction in plasma volume at age 80 years
C. a 40% reduction in functional hepatic tissue at age 80 years
D. a 30% reduction in renal function at aged 80 years
E. a reduction in MAC

Q1.55 In a 75-year-old male scheduled to undergo hemicolectomy, the following factors increase the risk of postoperative pulmonary complications:

A. a body mass index of 35
B. kyphoscoliosis
C. previous partial gastrectomy
D. epidural anaesthesia
E. poorly controlled postoperative pain

Q1.56 An anaphylactic reaction to thiopentone:

A. is preceded by pain on injection
B. is more common in patients with pre-existing asthma or eczema
C. is associated with severe bronchodilatation
D. is not necessarily mediated via IgE
E. must be immediately treated with intravenous adrenaline

Q1.57 Awareness during anaesthesia:

A. may result in increased oesophageal contractility
B. can be reliably indicated by changes in physiological parameters
C. is frequently due to faulty anaesthetic technique
D. may result in longterm stress, even if not consciously remembered
E. is best identified by bispectral analysis

Q1.58 Complications associated with invasive monitoring techniques include:

A. median nerve damage with brachial artery cannulation
B. arterio–venous fistula formation following radial artery cannulation
C. puncture of the internal carotid with right internal jugular line insertion
D. trauma to the thoracic duct following right internal jugular cannulation
E. thrombosis following femoral venous line insertion

Q1.59 The following are contraindications to epidural anaesthesia:

A. patient refusal
B. uncontrolled haemorrhage
C. known difficult intubation
D. pyrexia of 38.5°C associated with purulent sputum
E. inability to gain vascular access

Q1.60 The following conditions may be associated with instability of the cervical spine:

A. Down's syndrome
B. Paget's disease
C. rheumatoid arthritis
D. ankylosing spondylitis
E. cervical vertebral metastases

Q1.61 The clinical signs of raised intracranial pressure may include:

A. severe frontal headache, worse on standing
B. hypotension and bradycardia
C. nausea and vomiting
D. hyperventilation secondary to metabolic acidosis
E. diabetes mellitus

Q1.62 The risk of aspiration of gastric contents may be increased by:

A. diabetes mellitus
B. trauma
C. pyloric stenosis
D. suxamethonium
E. lithotomy postion

Q1.63 Complications associated with percutaneous tracheostomy performed in the intensive care unit include:

A. pneumomediastinum
B. tracheo–innominate fistula
C. tracheal stenosis
D. tracheal perforation
E. upper airway obstruction

Q1.64 The normal physiological autoregulation of cerebral perfusion pressure may be impaired by:

A. sevoflurane
B. trauma
C. seizures
D. hypoxia
E. hypertension

Q1.65 Hypotension during spinal anaesthesia may be due to:

A. vasoconstriction
B. dorsal root block
C. pre-ganglionic autonomic blockade
D. bradycardia
E. blockade of nerves supplying the adrenal medulla

Q1.66 Dystrophia myotonica is:

A. transmitted as a sex-linked recessive gene
B. associated with a life expectancy of approximately 40 years
C. a contraindication for the use of suxamethonium
D. associated with diabetes mellitus and cataracts
E. associated with hyperkalaemia

Q1.67 Neuromuscular blockade may be assumed to be adequately antagonised if the patient can:

A. lift his head from the pillow for 3 seconds
B. cough effectively
C. squeeze the nurses hand
D. open his eyes widely
E. maintain his arterial saturation above 95% on 4 litres min^{-1} of oxygen

Q1.68 A six-week-old male infant presents with a history of projectile vomiting and a palpable tumour in the epigastrium. The following statements are true:

A. associated cardiac lesions are probable
B. surgery is required immediately to relieve the obstruction
C. hyperkalaemia is probable
D. hypochloraemic acidosis may be present
E. severe hypovolaemia may be present

Q1.69 The following statements are true of acute epiglotitis:

A. only occurs in children
B. nasotracheal intubation is essential as children tolerate oral tubes poorly
C. if the diagnosis is suspected a throat swab should be taken and intravenous antibiotics should be given immediately
D. a lateral x-ray of the neck is useful to confirm the diagnosis
E. the incidence has decreased in the UK since the introduction of the MMR vaccine

Q1.70 Significant glycosuria may be associated with:

A. pregnancy
B. Fanconi's syndrome
C. Zollinger–Ellison syndrome
D. carcinoid syndrome
E. phaeochromocytoma

Q1.71 In a patient with ischaemic heart disease undergoing coronary artery bypass grafting, the following factors indicate an increased risk of perioperative morbidity or mortality:

A. female gender
B. myocardial infarction within the last six months
C. associated mitral regurgitation
D. a gallop rhythm
E. left main stem artery disease

Q1.72 In the statistical analysis of data:

A. nominal data is described by the mean and standard deviation
B. normally distributed data is described by the median and percentiles
C. a chi-squared test is appropriate to compare non-parametric nominal data
D. Student's *t*-test is applied to non-parametric ordinal data
E. a Type I error is a false positive

Q1.73 In relation to audit within the Anaesthetics Department:

A. when planning any audit a power analysis should be carried out
B. pre-operative starvation and unplanned postoperative admissions to ICU should be regularly audited
C. benchmarking allows new treatments to be validated
D. audit data must reach statistical significance to be useful
E. critical incident monitoring should be audited routinely

Q1.74 The following are reported in the annual SHOT (Serious Hazards of Transfusion) report:

A. post-transfusion pyrexia greater than 38.5°C
B. transfusion-related lung injury
C. transfusion of an incorrect component of blood if no harm has been caused to the patient
D. post-transfusion purpura
E. transfusion-related renal failure

Q1.75 Latex allergy may be characterised by:

A. urticaria
B. rhinitis
C. conjunctivitis
D. dyspnoea
E. anaphylaxis

Q1.76 Evidence of the following complications of central venous cannulation may be present on a posterior–anterior chest x-ray:

A. intra-arterial placement
B. right atrial perforation
C. air embolism
D. extrapleural haemorrhage
E. knotted catheter

Q1.77 A 73-year-old woman with known hypothyroidism is admitted to the intensive care unit. The following are consistent with a diagnosis of myxodema coma:

A. acute confusional state
B. hyperpyrexia
C. tachycardia
D. seizures
E. ileus

Answers to Section 1

Q1.1
A = True
B = False
C = True
D = True
E = True

In a conscious patient, e.g. during hip replacement under regional anaesthesia, venous air embolism may be characterised by coughing, chest pain and dyspnoea. In the anaesthetised patient, signs include tachycardia and cardiac arrhythmias, including ventricular fibrillation. A decrease in end tidal carbon dioxide, arterial oxygen tension and cardiac output also occurs. The reduction in end tidal carbon dioxide is an early sign and is often sudden, reflecting the increase in pulmonary dead space and the associated decrease in cardiac output. Bronchospasm, pulmonary oedema, raised pulmonary artery pressure and pulmonary artery resistance and right-sided strain on the ECG may also occur. On auscultation, tinkling sounds may be heard or, in the presence of large amounts of air, the classical 'mill-wheel' murmur may be heard over the prechordium. This is generally a late sign, which is often preceded by circulatory collapse. A machinery murmur is characteristic of a patent ductus arteriosus.

Q1.2
A = False
B = False
C = True
D = False
E = False

A child with post-tonsillectomy bleeding presents the anaesthetist with a combination of problems. The child has a potentially difficult airway (the presence of blood and the possibility of significant post-intubation oedema), cardiovascular compromise and residual anaesthesia. Resuscitation should begin immediately on the ward with intravenous fluids (isotonic salt solutions or colloids, *not* dextrose solutions) in $20\,ml\,kg^{-1}$ boluses. A blood sample should be sent for urgent cross-match, full blood count and clotting profile. Senior assistance should be available. When cardiovascular stability is achieved, anaesthesia may be induced using intravenous or inhalational induction. It is advisable to empty the stomach of blood before emergence from anaesthesia using a wide bore orogastric tube placed under direct vision by the surgeon and removed before the patient wakes.

Q1.3
A = True
B = True
C = False
D = False
E = True

Acute urinary retention may occur postoperatively, particularly following pelvic or perineal surgery. It may be associated with the pre-existence of benign prostatic hypertrophy, the use of spinal or epidural opioids, or following the administration of drugs with anticholinergic effects. Neurological causes are less common but include autonomic neuropathy, including that associated with diabetes mellitus. Urinary retention may result in agitation and confusion, particularly in the elderly, and can cause hypertension, tachycardia and raised intracranial pressure. In addition to the associated clinical signs, urinary catheterisation will differentiate between acute urinary retention and oliguria secondary to hypovolaemia or hypotension.

Q1.4
A = False
B = False
C = True
D = False
E = True

Laser (<u>L</u>ight <u>A</u>mplification by the <u>S</u>timulated <u>E</u>mission of <u>R</u>adiation) surgery is performed using a beam of light of single wavelength in which all the waves are in phase at any one time, i.e. they are monochromatic and coherent. There are three principle types of laser used in medicine, named after the substance that emits the light: argon, neodymium-yttrium aluminium garnet (Nd-Yag), and carbon dioxide. These can produce intense local heat which may be used to coagulate or cauterise, or even to cut tissues like a scalpel. The power and application of a laser is dependent upon its wavelength and its power density. Both Nd-Yag and carbon dioxide lasers may be used in laser surgery of the airway. The Nd-Yag laser may be used to debulk bronchial carcinomata and other tumours, and the carbon dioxide laser has a wide range of applications in ENT surgery, either for precise cutting or coagulation.

The use of lasers in the airway presents the anaesthetist with a number of problems in addition to those associated with a shared airway. The most important of these is the risk of explosion. During surgery of the airway, the laser beam may cause ignition of the endotracheal tube, anaesthetic gases or even the surgical drapes. If an endotracheal tube is necessary it must be shielded from the laser. PVC, silicone or rubber tubes may rapidly melt, allowing the oxygen-rich anaesthetic gases to ignite. Specific laser-proof tubes may be used. These may be made of flexible stainless steel, or may be PVC tubes which have been coated with a layer of teflon, aluminium and silicone during manufacture. If a cuffed tube is used the cuff should be filled with saline rather than air so that if the cuff bursts it may be easily detected and the saline will absorb some of the laser energy. Alternatively an endotracheal tube with a foam-filled cuff specifically for use in laser surgery of the airway is available.

Oxygen and nitrous oxide will support combustion, therefore the use of low concentrations of oxygen is advocated (e.g. less than 40% oxygen in either helium or nitrogen). In order to further limit the risk of airway explosions the laser is used in bursts of less than 10 seconds in duration rather than in a continual stream.

If an endotracheal tube is not required, or it is not practical when considered in relation to the pathology or the surgical requirements, supraglottic jet ventilation, transglottic catheter or transtracheal ventilation may be used. Intravenous anaesthesia is essential when jet ventilation is used, and relatively high infusion rates may be required to prevent awareness. Jet ventilation is not safe in the presence of an obstructed airway. If there is obstruction to the outflow of gases through the larynx, severe barotrauma may result.

Q1.5
A = False
B = False
C = False
D = True
E = False

A posteroanterior chest x-ray is a useful tool in detecting structural, as opposed to functional, abnormalities of the intrathoracic cardiorespiratory system. In an adult the heart shadow should represent less than 50% of the thoracic diameter; in the absence of disease this ratio does not increase with increasing age. If part of the heart border is indistinct, this may indicate adjacent pulmonary pathology. An indistinct right heart border suggests right middle lobe pathology, whereas an indistinct left heart border may indicate lingula pathology. The left hilum is usually one to two centimetres higher than the right due to the position of the heart predominantly in the left chest; conversely the right hemidiaphragm is usually two centimetres higher that the left due to the position of the liver. The azygos lobe, when present (0.5% of patients), occurs at the right apex and is formed by the embryological migration of the azygos vein with its fold of pleura from the chest wall to drain into the superior vena cava. Pneumothoraces, particularly when small, are easily missed on chest radiographs. If suspected, a chest x-ray on expiration should be specifically requested, as the pneumothorax will increase in size on expiration.

Q1.6
A = False
B = False
C = True
D = False
E = False

In 1998 the General Dental Council agreed that by 2001 all general anaesthetics for dental surgery must be given in hospital, by or under the supervision of an anaesthetist on the specialist register. The Association of Anaesthetists' guidance on minimum standards of monitoring must be adhered to and full resuscitation equipment including suction must be immediately available. Patients are usually admitted as day cases and therefore the anaesthetic management must follow usual day-care guidelines for preoperative investigation and discharge. Cardiac arrhythmias are common during dental extractions precipitated by high levels of circulating catecholamines, particularly if the patient is anxious. These may be exacerbated by hypercarbia and vagal stimulation. The incidence of arrhythmias is greatly increased by halothane, and is much less common with the newer agents such as sevoflurane or desflurane. Lignocaine may be infiltrated prior to dental surgery to reduce the incidence of arrhythmias.

Limited mouth opening or trismus may be due to dental infection resulting in masseter spasm. Other causes of trismus include fractured mandible, temperomandibular joint disease, parotitis, tetanus, cerebrovascular accident, strychnine poisoning, phenothiazines, the administration of suxamethonium in patients with dystrophia myotonica, malignant hyperpyrexia and hysteria. The trismus due to dental infection usually relaxes to some degree following induction of anaesthesia; however, this should not be relied upon and all patients with significant trismus should be regarded as a potential difficult laryngoscopy and intubation.

Q1.7
A = False
B = False
C = False
D = True
E = True

This patient presented with a low blood pressure and decreased cardiac output (normal range 2.8–4.2 litre min^{-1} m^{-2}) in the presence of high filling pressures, i.e. a central venous pressure of 14 mm Hg (normal range 0–8mmHg) and a pulmonary capillary wedge pressure of 22 mm Hg (normal range 6–15 mmHg). This suggests a diagnosis of cardiac failure, possibly secondary to perioperative myocardial infarction or fluid overload. Hypovolaemia and sepsis are unlikely at this stage, as the hypotension would be accompanied by low central venous and pulmonary capillary wedge pressures. The initial management of this patient should therefore include the administration of humidified oxygen via a facemask, urinary catheterisation and the commencement of inotropic support. Further investigation might include a twelve-lead ECG, urea and electrolyte, full blood count and blood gas analysis.

Q1.8
A = False
B = False
C = True
D = True
E = True

Awake endotracheal intubation is indicated in patients in whom intubation is suspected, or known, to be difficult, the cervical spine is unstable, or the isolation of lung segments prior to anaesthesia is essential, e.g. in bronchopleural fistula, tracheo-oesophageal fistula or occasionally in the presence of a full stomach. Although not mandatory, antisilagogues are recommended as premedication, as their drying effect improves the effectiveness of topically applied local anaesthetic agents. Awake tracheal intubation may be performed with local anaesthesia blind via the nasal approach, with conventional laryngoscopy, or with the aid of a fibreoptic bronchoscope.

Cocaine is an ester local anaesthetic agent found in the leaves and bark of the coca plant. It is a potent inhibitor of uptake −1 in noradrenergic nerve terminals and also inhibits monoamine oxidase, increasing the effects of sympathetic stimulation. This produces tachycardia, vasoconstriction, hypertension, cardiac dysrhythmias, coronary and cerebral thrombosis, heart failure and pyrexia, as well as acting as a central stimulant. Large doses may result in tremors, convulsions, coma, respiratory depression, pulmonary oedema, brochospasm and renal failure. Dependence is common. The maximum safe dose is 1.5 mg kg^{-1}; doses above 1 g are often fatal. Despite being a highly effective local anaesthetic agent, the number and significance of the side effects associated with cocaine usage mean that it is now no longer the drug of choice for nasal mucosal vasoconstriction and anaesthesia.

Nebulised lignocaine 4% may be used to anaesthetise the entire upper airway prior to awake intubation. This mode of administration has the additional benefit that the potentially toxic doses of lignocaine often inadvertently given during the spray-as-you-go technique may be avoided.

Q1.9
A = True
B = True
C = True
D = False
E = False

ARDS is a form of hypoxic respiratory failure resulting in diffuse alveolar damage. It has an incidence in the United Kingdom of approximately 5:100,000 and represents the most severe form of acute lung injury. It may be defined as acute lung injury with a PaO_2/F_1O_2 of less than 26.6 kPa. Common causes include sepsis, aspiration pneumonitis, trauma, massive blood transfusion and pancreatitis. There are three phases to the disease: an early exudative phase, a proliferative phase and a fibrotic phase. Treatment is largely supportive and should include deep vein thrombosis prophylaxis. Ventilatory management may include permissive hypercapnoea, reversal of the I:E ratio, inhaled nitric oxide and prone positioning. High levels of positive end expiratory pressure (PEEP) may be necessary. The administration of steroids remains controversial but they may be of benefit if the initial response to the above ventilatory strategies is not sustained. Acute sepsis must be excluded prior to commencing steroid therapy.

Q1.10
A = False
B = True
C = True
D = True
E = True

Congenital heart disease affects up to 0.8% of live births. Many of these defects are associated with a risk of bacterial endocarditis following invasive procedures in which the integrity of a mucosal surface is breached. These include dental and other intraoral treatment, gastrointestinal endoscopy, bronchoscopy, tonsillectomy and urinary catheterisation. Patients at highest risk include those who have prosthetic material within the heart such as a prosthetic valve, shunt or conduit, and those with a high velocity jet such as that arising from a ventricular septal defect, patent ductus arteriosus or stenotic aortic or mitral valve. Longterm antibiotic prophylaxis is recommended for most patients with congenital cardiac disease, with the exception of those who have undergone ligation of a patent ductus arteriosus or primary closure of a secundum atrial septal defect surgically. In these situations prophylaxis is only necessary for the six months following surgery. If a device has been used to close an ASD or PDA in the catheter lab, then, as foreign material is present in the heart, longterm antibiotic prophylaxis is required.

Innocent heart murmurs occur in over 50% of children and are not associated with any physiological or anatomical abnormality. Innocent murmurs usually occur in early to mid-systole, are short in duration and loudest in the supine position and on exercise. They never occur during diastole and by definition do not require antibiotic prophylaxis.

Q1.11
A = True
B = True
C = False
D = False
E = False

Preoxygenation following a mandibular fracture may be difficult as swelling is often substantial and there may be other associated facial fractures making it difficult to achieve a comfortable seal between the facemask and the face. Although many of these fractures are now plated, some still require intermaxillary fixation in the form of wires. Following wiring of the jaw these patients are often managed on a normal ward. Airway complications are uncommon; however, it is advisable always to have a set of wire cutters taped to the bed or wall within easy reach so that, in an emergency, the wires fixing the jaws together can be cut and the patient intubated if necessary. Despite the often substantial swelling, conventional laryngoscopy and intubation are usually possible. It is important, however, always to treat these patients as potential difficult intubations and ensure that additional equipment and help is immediately available in the event of difficulty.

Q1.12
A = False
B = True
C = True
D = True
E = False

Septic shock may be defined as sepsis associated with refractory hypotension and signs of poor perfusion despite adequate fluid resuscitation. The majority of cases are caused by bacterial infection, by both Gram-negative and Gram-positive organisms, and although in the early stages there may be an increase in cardiac output severe myocardial dysfunction may also occur. The resultant failure of peripheral perfusion leads to an increase in anaerobic metabolism and the production of lactate (normal value $0.6–1.8 \, \text{mmol litre}^{-1}$), the concentration of which has been shown to be inversely proportional to survival. Other complications associated with septic shock include acute respiratory distress syndrome, renal failure, hepatic failure, pancreatitis and disseminated intravascular coagulation.

Q1.13
A = False
B = False
C = True
D = True
E = False
Spinal cord injury occurs most commonly in young adult males aged 15–35 years, usually as a result of a road traffic accident. Injury at the level of the fifth and sixth cervical vertebrae is the most common site, followed by the lumbar spine. The thoracic spine is relatively rarely affected. Associated injury, most commonly head injury, may be present in up to 60% of cases. Acute spinal cord injury is characterised in the first instance by hypertension due to peripheral vasoconstriction or hypotension in the case of lesions above the level of T6 due to disruption of the sympathetic nerve supply. Initially flaccid paralysis occurs, to be followed by increasing spasticity after two to three weeks. Arrhythmias are common with bradycardias predominating in lesions above T1 due to unopposed vagal activity. Neurogenic pulmonary oedema is a common complication of cervical cord damage and may be dramatic. The anaesthetic management of these patients must include meticulous attention to the airway and adequacy of the breathing. Intubation is indicated if the airway is not maintainable by other means, or if the breathing is inadequate due to a lesion above the level of the phrenic nerve (C3–C5) or an associated head injury with a Glasgow Coma Score of less than 8. Fibreoptic intubation is not the method of choice; intubation can usually be more rapidly and safely achieved in the presence of an unstable cervical spine by the rigorous use of manual in-line cervical stabilisation.

Q1.14
A = False
B = False
C = False
D = True
E = False
In the anaesthetic management of phaeochromocytoma, preoperative α-blockade is essential in order to reverse the peripheral vasoconstriction and resultant intravascular depletion secondary to high circulating levels of catecholamines. Phenoxybenzamine is the drug of choice as it is a long acting α-blocker which binds irreversibly with the α-receptors. Conversely phenylephrine is an α-agonist and is therefore absolutely contraindicated. β-blockade may also be added if there is a persistent tachycardia, but is not mandatory. Pancuronium should be avoided as it may precipitate a tachy-

cardia via its sympathomimetic effects. Postoperatively, approximately 50% of patients remain hypertensive for 1–3 days. The majority of patients also have a degree of preoperative and intraoperative hyperglycaemia as the circulating catecholamines suppress insulin release. However, within minutes of the removal of the tumour this suppression of β-cell function disappears, the plasma insulin level rises, and severe hypoglycaemia may result. Thus glucose-containing fluids should be infused following removal of the tumour and the blood glucose level carefully monitored in the postoperative period.

Q1.15
A = False
B = False
C = True
D = False
E = False

The correct size, in mm, of tracheal tube for a child can be estimated from the formula (age/4)+4; however, this is only a guide and a tube should be chosen that allows a small leak around the tube and ensures adequate ventilation. Usually plain tracheal tubes are used, but small, cuffed tubes are available and are useful in selected situations such as on intensive care in a child who proves difficult to ventilate because of poor compliance. If used, the cuff must be carefully positioned below the cricoid cartilage to avoid damage at this, the narrowest part of the larynx. The size approximates to the size of the child's fifth finger, a rough guide which is particularly useful in the acute arrest situation. The length can be estimated as about three times the internal diameter of the tube, and the position must be checked by auscultation to ensure both sides of the chest are equally ventilated. Nasal tubes can be used in all age groups and are often better tolerated than oral tubes if longer-term use is required.

Q1.16
A = False
B = True
C = False
D = False
E = True

Children have on average between two and nine upper respiratory tract infections per year. If the child appears well and symptoms are mild with no systemic upset, the anaesthesia may not be associated with any increase in perioperative risk. Children with high fevers, who are miserable or lethargic or who have chest signs, should not undergo elective surgery. Children under 1 year of age are most at risk of airway complications such as cough, bronchospasm, desaturation or stridor perioperatively. Those who have had a recent infection are most at risk.

Healthy children undergoing surgery not anticipated to involve significant blood loss do not require preoperative haemoglobin measurements. The most likely cause of mild anaemia in children is dietary iron deficiency.

The sickledex is a rapid screening test for the presence of HbS. In young infants with high levels of HbF (particularly those under 3 months of age) the test can be misleading, as HbS levels, though present, are not high enough to provide a positive test. A haemoglobin electrophoresis will correctly identify the haemoglobin pattern in all age groups.

Q1.17
A = True
B = False
C = True
D = True
E = True

A high central venous pressure in the presence of acute circulatory failure indicates either heart failure or right ventricular outflow tract obstruction with either clot, air, amniotic fluid or an increase in pulmonary vascular resistance secondary to lung collapse.

Q1.18
A = False
B = True
C = False
D = True
E = False

Compared to adults, babies less than 28 days old (neonates) have a higher oxygen consumption ($3\,ml\,kg^{-1}\,min^{-1}$ in an adult, $6\,ml\,kg^{-1}\,min^{-1}$ in a neonate). The blood volume of a neonate is approximately $85\,ml\,kg^{-1}$, $80\,ml\,kg^{-1}$ in a child and $75\,ml\,kg^{-1}$ in an adult. Hypoglycaemia is dangerous in neonates and is associated with fitting and the risk of cerebral damage. Frequent blood sugar estimates should be done perioperatively and small babies may require 10% or 20% dextrose as maintenance fluid to prevent hypoglycaemia. Neonates lose heat easily and have difficulty maintaining their body temperature as they have immature responses, cannot shiver and vasoconstrict poorly. The critical temperature (i.e. the temperature below which the naked subject can maintain its body temperature) is 23°C in the neonate and 6°C in the adult.

Q1.19
A = True
B = True
C = False
D = False
E = True

Ischaemia, secondary to atherosclerosis in the transplanted heart, may occur, and may be painless making diagnosis difficult. Routine coronary angiography is undertaken following transplantation in order to assess the coronaries. The survival rate following heart transplantation is currently above 70% at 5 years. Survival rates for patients who have had lung transplants are considerably less at approximately 50% at 5 years. The transplanted heart will respond to endogenous circulating catecholamines and exogenous catecholamines. It does not retain any intrinsic sympathetic or parasympathetic supply. Early complications following renal transplantation include bleeding, pain, hypertension and oliguria associated with a degree of acute tubular damage and thrombosis of the vascular anastomoses and rejection. Patients who have had bone marrow transplants receive irradiated and filtered blood due to the risk of precipitating graft-versus-host disease if they are exposed to sensitising white blood cells.

Q1.20
A = True
B = True
C = True
D = True
E = True

This is a reliable method of blocking the brachial plexus (and is associated with a low incidence of complications). The subclavian perivascular block involves inserting a needle where the interscalene groove crosses the subclavian artery and advancing it in a caudal direction. Hoarseness may result from a temporary block of the recurrent laryngeal nerve producing a vocal cord palsy. This requires no treatment, but bilateral blocks should never be undertaken. The risk of bilateral phrenic nerve blocks or bilateral pneumothoraces is also a potent reason for avoiding bilateral blocks.

Q1.21
A = True
B = True
C = True
D = False
E = False

Reflex sympathetic dystrophy (RSD) is a chronic pain condition that may develop after apparently minor injury. It is characterised by a burning pain limiting movement, hyperalgesia, skin changes in the affected area and typical changes of demineralisation on the bone scan. It occurs in children and adults. It appears that injury causes overgrowth of the noradrenergic sympathetic nerves so that sympathetic stimulation results in pain. Guanethidine acts to block the release of noradrenaline from the post-ganglionic adrenergic neurone and also depletes the nerve endings of noradrenaline. In RSD it has been used as regular intravenous injections in the affected limb (isolated by use of a tourniquet cuff) over a course of several weeks. Opiates are ineffective in this condition.

Q1.22
A = True
B = False
C = True
D = True
E = False

N-Methyl-D-aspartate receptors are present in neurones, particularly in the hippocampus. They are present at presynaptic afferent nerve endings. Ketamine is an antagonist at the NMDA receptors. Gamma amino butyric acid is a significant inhibitory neurotransmitter in the brain. Benzodiazepines act at this site to reduce anxiety and produce muscle relaxation. They do not have a particular role in pain pathways. Dorsal column stimulators implanted in the epidural space can be very useful in the management of chronic pain states. Behavioural modification and training is used successfully in many patients.

The mu_2 receptor is mainly the site of action producing the respiratory, cardiovascular and gastrointestinal effects of opiates. Analgesic activity is mainly at the mu_1 delta and kappa receptors. Opioid receptors have recently been reclassified as OP1 (delta), OP2 (kappa) and OP3 (mu).

Q1.23
A = False
B = True
C = False
D = False
E = True

Opiates do not affect platelet function. Non-steroidal anti-inflammatory agents do affect platelet function by reducing platelet aggregation, which may be important in major surgery. Although longterm use of non-steroidal anti-inflammatory agents is associated with gastric irritation and an increased risk of gastric ulceration, they do not delay emptying. The speed of action of a drug given intrathecally is directly proportional to the drug's lipid solubility. Fentanyl is more lipophilic than morphine. Morphine is more hydrophilic, so it tends remain within the CSF for a longer period of time. Pethidine is metabolised in the liver but the metabolite norpethidine may accumulate and produce neurotoxicity. This metabolite is mildly analgesic and also has convulsive properties. It tends to accumulate in patients with renal failure.

Q1.24
A = False
B = False
C = True
D = False
E = False

Local anaesthesia to the brachial plexus, via the axillary approach, is a useful block for hand and forearm surgery. Alternatives are the interscalene and the subclavicular approach to the brachial plexus. The axillary approach has the lowest incidence of pneumothorax. A transarterial approach is commonly used. The needle passes through the artery and the local anaesthetic is deposited posteriorly, the needle is withdrawn anterior to the artery, and the remaining local anaesthetic instilled. The block may last many hours. It is suitable for adults and children. Complications include the risk of intravascular injection and, rarely, neuropathy may result secondary to direct trauma to the plexus. The risk is decreased when a nerve stimulator is used in the awake patient.

Q1.25
A = True
B = False
C = True
D = True
E = True

The coeliac plexus contains sympathetic and parasympathetic input from T5 to T12 and the vagus. The two coeliac ganglia lie retroperitoneally just below the diaphragm and both need to be blocked. Diagnostic blocks are done with local anaesthetic, but for terminal cancer pain a destructive block with alcohol is used.

Carbamazepine, phenytoin and sodium valproate have been used effectively in chronic pain syndromes (such as trigeminal neuralgia). Transcutaneous nerve stimulation is not used in trigeminal neuralgia, which is more commonly managed with either antiepiteptic drugs or destruction of the ganglia or surgical decompression. Epidurally administered corticosteroids are used successfully in the management of some chronic back pain syndromes, but they may be associated with local irritation and arachnoiditis. Antidepressant drugs are used in many chronic pain syndromes. They act to decrease anxiety and depression and improve sleep patterns.

Q1.26
A = True
B = True
C = False
D = True
E = True
The stellate ganglion is formed by the fusion of the seventh and eighth cervical and first thoracic sympathetic ganglia. It lies anterior to the lateral process of C7 and T1. Successful blockade results in interruption of the sympathetic supply to the ipsilateral face and arm. This is indicated by meiosis, ptosis, enophthalmos, conjunctival vasodilitation and unilateral nasal congestion (Horner syndrome).

Q1.27
A = True
B = True
C = True
D = True
E = False
Many painful conditions are associated with overactivity of the sympathetic nervous system, therefore sympathetic blockade may be used either diagnostically or therapeutically. It is used in reflex sympathetic dystrophy as a course of guanethidine blocks. In peripheral vascular disease, sympathetic blockade is particularly useful in decreasing rest pain, and it may also aid the healing of ischaemic ulcers. It does not help with diabetic neuropathy. Stellate ganglion block may be of value following inadvertent intra-arterial injection of thiopentone, as it will decrease vascular spasm. Sympathetic blocks help hyperhidrosis only temporarily, and surgical sympathectomy offers a more permanent solution.

Q1.28
A = True
B = False
C = True
D = True
E = True
The prolonged administration of nitrous oxide results in a reduction of the

synthesis of vitamin B_{12}, a co-enzyme for methionine synthetase which is essential for DNA synthesis. Twenty-four hours of continuous administration of nitrous oxide results in megaloblastic changes in the bone marrow. Other haematological effects of prolonged nitrous oxide include anaemia, leucopenia and thrombocytopenia. A peripheral neuropathy may occur with chronic abuse. Nitrous oxide does not affect hepatic or renal function or skeletal muscle tone.

Q1.29
A = True
B = True
C = True
D = True
E = True

Aspiration, multiple fractures, pulmonary contusion, massive blood transfusion and persistent hypotension are all risk factors for developing Acute Respiratory Distress Syndrome following trauma. The risk is said to be 18% if one risk factor is present, 42% if two factors are present and 85% if three are present.

Q1.30
A = True
B = False
C = False
D = True
E = False

The Trauma Score is a scoring system used in triage and as a predictor of outcome. It is based on five variables: the Glasgow Coma Score, the systolic blood pressure, the respiratory rate and effort and capillary refill. Each parameter is awarded points to give a best-possible total of 16. It is recommended that all patients with a score less than 12 should be transferred to a trauma centre for treatment.

As capillary refill and respiratory effort may be difficult to assess in the trauma setting, these have been dropped in the Revised Trauma Score, which is therefore solely based upon the Glasgow Coma Score, the systolic blood pressure and the respiratory rate. Each of these three parameters is then coded and weighted, and their sum gives the Revised Trauma Score with a possible score of between 0 and 7.8408. Heaviest weighting is given to the Glasgow Coma Score, in order to identify those patients with severe head injury but little disturbance in the cardiovascular or respiratory systems. The higher the Revised Trauma Score, the better the prognosis.

The score has been modified further for use in paediatrics, assigning scores of −1 to +2 according to the size of the child, airway patency, systolic blood pressure, consciousness level, type of fracture and cutaneous injury. It is recommended that all children with a Paediatric Trauma Score of less than 8 should be treated in a trauma centre.

Q1.31
A = False
B = True
C = False
D = False
E = False

A retrobulbar block requires supplementation with a facial nerve block and conjuctival anaesthesia in order to provide effective anaesthesia of the globe. An effective retrobulbar block requires a less-than-5 ml solution of local anaesthetic injected via a 3 cm needle which is inserted through the conjunctiva at the lower lateral orbital rim. The needle is advanced backwards and 10° superiorly until the tip passes the widest diameter of the eye and is then angled medially and upwards until the tip reaches a position behind the globe at the level of the iris, around 2 cm from the conjunctiva. The needle should then be aspirated and 2–4 ml of lignocaine with hyaluronidase injected. This results in pupillary dilatation, a reduction of intraocular pressure, and paralysis of the extraocular muscles. Complications include retrobulbar haemorrhage and subarachnoid injection leading to cardiorespiratory collapse. Perforation of the sclera may be detected by observing rotation of the globe, and is more likely when the axial length of the globe is greater than 2.6 cm.

The potential severity of the complications associated with retrobulbar block has increased the use of the peribulbar block. In the latter the local anaesthetic is injected outside the cone of ocular muscles, thus the risk of haemorrhage is minimal and there is no need for supplementation with a facial nerve block. A peribulbar block may be achieved by injecting 3–4 ml of local anaesthetic via a needle inserted to a depth of 2–2.5 cm through the lid margin between the supraorbital notch and the inner canthus of the eye and directed superiorly between the globe and the orbital roof. A separate injection is then made at the junction between the inner two thirds and the outer third of the lower lid. The needle is directed inferiorly between the globe and the orbital floor, and again 4–5 ml of local anaesthetic is injected at a depth of 2–2.5 cm. A mixture of 2% lignocaine and 0.5% bupivacaine is commonly used. Firm pressure is then applied to the eye for around 10 minutes while the block develops. Bradycardia is more common than tachycardia during the performance of an ophthalmic block due to stimulation of the oculocardiac reflex. The incidence of bradycardia may be reduced by the use of an anticholinergic premedicant.

Q1.32
A = True
B = False
C = True
D = False(True)
E = True

Infections which have been transmitted from donor to recipient via a blood transfusion include hepatitis B, hepatitis C, human immunodeficiency virus, cytomegalovirus, Epstein Barr virus, toxoplasmosis, malaria and syphilis. Hepatitis A is transmitted via contaminated waste, and to date there are no reports of variant Creutzfeldt-Jakob disease (variant CJD) having been transmitted via blood transfusion in humans.

Q1.33
A = True
B = True
C = True
D = True
E = False

Complications due to transoesophageal echocardiography are relatively rare, occurring in less than 1% of cases. They may be divided into complications due to direct mechanical trauma, displacement of or traction on adjacent structures, and stimulation of visceral reflexes. Direct mechanical trauma may occur on insertion, manipulation and removal of the probe and includes chipped teeth, pharyngeal abrasion, oesophageal rupture or haemorrhage, or rupture of a dissecting aortic aneurysm. Traction on adjacent structures includes laryngeal nerve damage resulting in transient vocal cord palsy. During transoesophageal echocardiography under general anaesthesia, the recurrent laryngeal nerve may be similarly damaged as it may be trapped between the probe and the endotracheal tube. Unwanted visceral reflexes stimulated by transoesophageal echocardiography include laryngospasm, bronchospasm, vomiting, arrhythmias, hypertension and myocardial ischaemia in patients with coronary artery disease. There are no reports of subsequent pharyngeal pouch development after the performance of a transoesophageal echocardiographic study, although the presence of a pharyngeal pouch is a relative contraindication to performing such a study as it may predispose to oesophageal rupture.

Q1.34
A = False
B = False
C = True
D = False
E = True

Oesophageal intubation is not uncommon. A high level of vigilance is necessary in order to detect it so that the tube may be rapidly removed and replaced in the trachea. Reliable indicators of the correct placement of an endotracheal tube include direct visualisation of the endotracheal tube passing through the cords, fibreoptic bronchoscopy, and the presence and persistence of appropriate levels of end tidal carbon dioxide. A posterior–anterior chest x-ray cannot confirm the position of the tube as the oesophagus is situated immediately behind the trachea. A chest x-ray is often taken following intubation in order to confirm the correct length of the tube rather than whether it is sited in the trachea. Similarly, the presence of moisture within the tube and bilateral breath sounds are not reliable indicators that the tube is in the trachea. It is possible to hear bilateral breath sounds following an oesophageal intubation; as the stomach is ventilated, it dilates and the diaphragms are pushed upwards causing apparent breath sounds. In this situation oesophageal intubation may be excluded by listening with a stethoscope over the stomach; if gurgling sounds are heard in time with ventilation it is likely that the oesophagus has been intubated.

Q1.35
A = False
B = True
C = False
D = True
E = True

In the supine position the intracranial pressure (defined as the pressure exerted by the CSF in the frontal horns of the lateral ventricles) is normally 1–2 kPa. Raised intracranial pressure has many causes, including cerebral oedema, tumour, abscess, haematoma, hydrocephalus, impaired venous drainage and increased cerebral blood flow. Treatment of a raised intracranial pressure includes intermittent positive pressure ventilation to achieve an arterial PCO_2 of 4.0–4.5 kPa. In the past it was recommended that hyperventilation to even lower levels of PCO_2 should be performed in order to promote maximal cerebral vasoconstriction thus decreasing the volume of space within the cranium occupied by blood. However, it became apparent that such vigorous vasoconstriction may also critically reduce cerebral oxygen delivery and was probably only effective for 24–48 hours. Most anaesthetic agents including thiopentone, etomidate, propofol and benzo-diazepines reduce intracranial pressure, the exception being ketamine. Frusemide and mannitol reduce intracranial pressure by causing cerebral dehydration, and steroids may reduce the swelling and inflammation associated with intracranial tumours. Positive end expiratory pressure may cause a rise in intracranial pressure by impeding venous return.

Q1.36
A = True
B = True
C = False
D = False
E = False

Adequate preoxygenation prior to anaesthesia correlates with the denitrogenation of the lungs, i.e. the replacement of nitrogen with oxygen. Many studies indicate that breathing 100% oxygen via a close-fitting anaesthetic mask and circuit for three minutes with normal tidal volumes will result in the same partial pressure of oxygen in the blood at the time of tracheal intubation as will be achieved after similar breathing for five minutes. Also there is no significant difference between these PaO_2 values and those obtained after breathing 100% oxygen with four vital capacity breaths over 30 seconds.

Q1.37
A = True
B = False
C = False
D = True
E = True

Malignant hyperpyrexia has an incidence of 1:5000–1:200,000 patients. Inheritance is autosomal-dominant with variable penetrance, and in 50%–70% of affected families the gene responsible is on the long arm of chromosome 19 close to the gene regulating a receptor for the T tubule/sarcoplasmic reticulum in skeletal muscle. However, other genes on other chromosomes have also been implicated in a significant proportion of cases. Malignant hyperpyrexia should be suspected if there is masseter spasm after the administration of suxamethonium, or there is an unexplained unexpected tachycardia in association with an unexplained unexpected increase in end tidal carbon dioxide concentration. The temperature may rise in excess of 2°C per hour, and dantrolene, a muscle relaxant which inhibits the release of calcium from the sarcoplasmic reticulum, should be given early in a dose of 1 mg kg^{-1} and repeated as necessary up to total dose of 10 mg kg^{-1}. The differential diagnosis for malignant hyperpyrexia should include neuroleptic malignant syndrome and recreational drug use, such as Ecstasy.

Q1.38
A = False
B = True
C = False
D = True
E = False

In adults the commonest rhythm associated with cardiac arrest is ventricular fibrillation. In order to maximise the chance of survival, a shock must be delivered promptly; the chances of successful defibrillation decrease by 7%–10% every minute that ventricular fibrillation is allowed to persist. Thus up to three asynchronous shocks of 200 J, 200 J, 360 J are given as soon as possible. If this fails to terminate the ventricular fibrillation the trachea should be intubated, intravenous access sought and external cardiac compressions performed at a rate of 100 compressions per minute. Ventilation should be continued at a rate of approximately 12 breaths per minute. It is important that the chest compressions should not pause for ventilation in order to avoid a substantial fall in coronary perfusion pressure. Amiodarone should be considered in refractory ventricular fibrillation and may be given as early as before the delivery of the fourth shock, providing that it does not delay this shock. In persistent ventricular fibrillation the position of the paddles may be changed to anterior–posterior. This may result in successful defibrillation; however, there is no evidence that this position is any more successful than the conventional position.

Q1.39
A = True
B = True
C = True
D = False
E = True

In a patient with a permanent pacemaker it is important during the preoperative visit to:
i.   determine the reason for pacing
ii. assess whether the patient is pacemaker-dependent
iii. ensure that the pacemaker has been checked annually
iv. assess the severity of any associated cardiac disease
v.   check the serum electrolytes especially the potassium and magnesium levels.
   If surgically possible, diathermy should be avoided; it affects pacemakers

in three ways: the diathermy may directly damage the pacemaker if it is applied close to the pacemaker, ventricular fibrillation may be induced if the diathermy current is channelled along the pacemaker lead, and the myocardium at the tip of the lead may be subject to burning rendering subsequent pacing ineffective. If diathermy is essential, bipolar diathermy should be used, the indifferent plate must be attached with care and the diathermy use should be minimised by using short bursts at the lowest effective power output possible. The diathermy should not be used within 15 cm of the pacemaker and the indifferent plate should be as far away from the pacemaker and as close to the cutting blade as possible. The direction of current flow, i.e. from the blade to the plate, should be at right angles to that of the pacemaker system. Similarly, suxamethonium should be avoided in patients who are pacemaker-dependent as severe fasciculations may be interpreted as myocardial activity and inhibit some older types of pacemaker. If the pacemaker fails in a patient who is pacemaker-dependent, the drug of choice is currently isoprenaline.

Q1.40
A = False
B = True
C = False
D = True
E = True

Intraocular pressure is normally between 1.3 and 2.0 kPa, and is measured by assessing corneal indentation by a weighted plunger or by use of a puff of air. Factors which may increase intraocular pressure include external pressure on the eye, retrobulbar haematoma, hypercapnoea, hypoxia, hypertension, raised central venous pressure (due to coughing, vomiting, Trendelenburg position), and drugs such as sulphur hexafluoride, nitrous oxide, ketamine and suxamethonium. Factors which may decrease intraocular pressure include the administration of acetazolamine, mannitol, propofol, etomidate, thiopentone, benzodiazepines and all volatile agents.

Q1.41
A = False
B = False
C = True
D = True
E = True

The Royal College of Radiologists' guidelines for indications for a preoperative chest x-ray in patients undergoing elective non-cardiopulmonary surgery include:

i.   patients with acute respiratory symptoms, including chest pain
ii. recent immigrants from areas in which TB remains endemic and recent chest films are not available
iii. patients with possible metastases
iv. patients with established or suspected cardiorespiratory disease who have not had a chest x-ray in the last 12 months.

In addition, a chest x-ray is also recommended in patients undergoing cardiopulmonary surgery or investigation for:
i.   chest trauma
ii. biopsy localisation
iii. foreign body inhalation.

Age over 60 and a history of cigarette smoking alone are not indications for the performance of a preoperative chest x-ray. Unnecessary testing is expensive, time-consuming and may pose a small risk to the patient.

Q1.42
A = False
B = True
C = False
D = True
E = False

Absolute indications for the placement of a double-lumen endobroncheal tube include:
i.   in order to protect the healthy lung from potential soiling which may occur during haemoptysis, bronchiectasis, lung abscess, empyaema with a bronchopleural fistula or a tracheo-oesophageal fistula
ii. the management of a gas leak, e.g. giant lung cyst, bronchpleuro-cutaneous fistula, aquired tracheo-oesophageal fistula, tracheobronchial rupture and bronchoplastic surgery.

Relative indications for the placement of a double-lumen endobroncheal tube to improve surgical access include pulmonary surgery, oesophageal surgery, anterior spinal surgery and great vessel surgery.

Q1.43
A = True
B = False
C = True
D = False
E = False

For the diagnosis of brain stem death to be made in the United Kingdom, the patient must be unconscious, requiring ventilation and have a diagnosed condition known to cause brain stem death. Before formal testing can be carried out, there are certain conditions which must be met:

i.   there must be no depressant or relaxant drugs present (e.g. anaesthetic or neuromuscular blocking agents)
ii.   the patient must be normothermic (this may require active warming)
iii.   there should be no uncorrected metabolic or endocrine disturbance.

Brain stem tests should be carried out by two experienced doctors, at least one of whom should be a consultant. Neither should belong to the transplant team and both should have been registered for more than 5 years. The tests are performed twice; the time between the two sets of tests should be long enough to ensure that the non-functioning of the brainstem has persisted (usually 1–12 hours). The diagnosis of brain stem death is dependent upon the existence of no direct or consensual pupillary reaction to light, no corneal reflex, no motor response in the distribution of any cranial nerve to a painful stimulus (spinal reflexes are permissible), no oculovestibular response to 50ml of cold saline in the external auditory canal, and no cough or gag reflex. There must also be no efforts at spontaneous ventilation when the patient is disconnected from the ventilator and the $PaCO_2$ is allowed to rise to greater than 6.6kPa. Oxygenation must be maintained and saturations monitored throughout this period. The EEG and the doll's eye reflex are not part of the standard brain stem tests in this country.

Q1.44
A = True
B = True
C = True
D = True
E = False

Up to 15% of patients who suffer long bone fractures develop clinically significant fat embolism typically 1–3 days following the trauma. Clinical signs include confusion, restlessness, coma and convulsions, dyspnoea, cough, haemoptysis, hypoxemia, and pulmonary oedema, petechial rash over the trunk axillae and conjunctiva, tachycardia, hypotension, pyrexia, thrombocytopenia, hypocalcaemia and coagulapathy. Fat globules may be seen in the sputum and retinal blood vessels; however, the presence of fat droplets in the urine is a non-specific finding following trauma. The risk of fat embolism may be reduced by early correction of hypovolaemia, oxygen therapy and early fracture immobilisation. Once fat embolism is established, treatment is essentially supportive. Heparin, aprotinin, steroids, aspirin, prostacyclin and dextran have all be used in the management of fat embolism without any conclusive benefit.

Q1.45
A = True
B = False
C = False
D = True
E = False

According to the American Association of Blood Bank Guidelines, intra-operative cell salvage in adults is indicated:

i.   when the anticipated blood loss is greater than 20% of the patient's esti-mated blood volume
ii. when blood is routinely cross-matched for the procedure
iii. when more than 10% of patients undergoing the procedure require transfusion
iv. when the mean transfusion volume for the procedure is greater than one unit.

In addition, with the recent development of small-volume bowls, cell salvage may also be used in children as small as 10–12 kg. Following cell salvage the red cells are suspended in normal saline solution prior to reinfusion and may be acceptable to patients with a moral or religious objection to bank blood such as Jehovah's Witnesses; however, this must be confirmed by detailed discussion with the patient. If the red blood cells are inadequately washed during the cell salvage procedure, free haemoglobin released from damaged red blood cells may precipitate renal failure in susceptible individuals.

Q1.46
A = False
B = True
C = False
D = False
E = False

A litre of 5% dextrose contains 50g glucose. Hartmann's solution (Ringer's lactate) contains sodium chloride 131 mmol litre^{-1}, potassium 5 mmol litre^{-1}, calcium 2 mmol litre^{-1}, chloride 111 mmol litre^{-1} and lactate 29 mmol litre^{-1}. Haemaccel contains approximately 6.5 mmol litre^{-1} of calcium as well as gelatin (MW 35,000 daltons), sodium, potassium and chloride in similar concentrations to Hartmann's solution. It also contains trace amounts of phosphate and sulphate. Normal saline solution contains sodium 150 mmol litre^{-1} and chloride 150 mmol litre^{-1}. Hydroxyethyl starch solutions have a mean molecular weight of from 200,000 to 450,000 daltons.

Q1.47
A = True
B = True
C = True
D = True
E = True

Carbon monoxide binds avidly to haemoglobin with an affinity 250 times greater that that of oxygen, thus effectively reducing the oxygen-carrying capacity of the blood, in turn causing tissue hypoxia. Carbon monoxide poisoning is treated with high-inspired concentrations of oxygen, or even hyperbaric oxygen in very severe cases. In other conditions where there is a reduced oxygen-carrying capacity, e.g. major haemorrhage or tamponade, or there is a reduced uptake of oxygen from the lungs, e.g. pneumothorax or pneumonia, oxygen should form part of the supportive therapy in addition to definitive treatment. Conditions such as thyrotoxic crisis, malignant hyperpyrexia and severe sepsis are characterised by a markedly increased metabolic rate, thus increasing the tissue oxygen demand above the available normal oxygen delivery. Thus oxygen supplementation is again essential.

Q1.48
A = True
B = False
C = True
D = False
E = True

The administration of an epidural dose of local anaesthetic into the subarachnoid space results in the rapid onset of a dense motor block, often before any sympathetic block can be detected. The speed of onset, although not always its extension, is often rapid, and hypotension is also rapid and severe. Intubation and ventilation may be necessary, as patients usually require 1–2 hours of ventilatory support before they are able to maintain adequate spontaneous ventilation once more. The presence of a large dose of local anaesthetic within the CSF results in widely dilated pupils which return to normal as the block recedes; they do not necessarily indicate cerebral damage, although this may occur secondary to inadequately treated hypotension and apnoea. It is important to remember that a total spinal may also occur on topping up a previously satisfactory epidural. This is probably not due to the migration of the catheter, but to the initial placement of the multi-hole catheter partly within the subarachnoid space. An initial slow injection causes the local anaesthetic to emerge from the most proximal holes in the catheter, resulting in an effective epidural block, but a fast subsequent top-up may cause the majority of the solution to emerge from the distal holes resulting in a subarachnoid block.

Q1.49
A = False
B = False
C = True
D = False
E = True
There are several scoring systems available to aid the diagnosis of difficult intubation at the stage of the preoperative anaesthetic visit. Unfortunately they all lack sensitivity and specificity to a greater or lesser extent. The Mallampati classification grades the pharyngeal structures visible when the patient opens his mouth widely and protrudes his tongue. Grade III or higher predicts in the region of 50% of difficult intubations, with a high incidence of false positives. The Wilson score is based upon five risk factors: weight, head and neck movement, jaw movement, mandibular recession and the presence of buck teeth. Each factor has three possible scores (0–2) giving a maximum score of 10. A score of greater than 2 will predict 75% of difficult intubations, but again with a high number of false positives. Other factors known to correlate with difficult intubation include a thyromental distance of less than 6 cm, an inability to protrude the lower incisors in front of the upper incisors, a reduced atlanto–occipital distance, an increased posterior mandibular depth, and the ratio of the mandibular length to the posterior mandibular depth being greater than 3.6.

Q1.50
A = False
B = False
C = True
D = True
E = True
Amniotic fluid embolism has an associated mortality of 60%–80% and is responsible for up to 10% of all maternal deaths. It may occur at any stage during pregnancy and is traditionally thought to be associated with a disruption of the normal relationship between the chorioamniotic membrane and the uterine vasculature, allowing access of the amniotic fluid to the systemic circulation, although there may also be an allergic component. Amniotic fluid embolism presents with sudden dyspnoea, cough, cyanosis, shivering, vomiting, apnoea and shock. 10%–20% of patients have convulsions. Of those that survive the acute event, the majority develop a coagulapathy rapidly manifested by major uterine haemorrhage. Acute lung injury may also occur. Haemoptysis is associated with massive pulmonary embolism. Pregnancy-induced hypertension does not predispose to amniotic fluid embolism.

Q1.51
A = True
B = True
C = True
D = True
E = False
Obstructive sleep apnoea is associated with obesity, tonsillar hypertrophy, craniofacial abnormalities, acromegaly and hypothyroidism. Ventilation may be normal while awake, but during sleep (especially REM sleep) the decreased upper airway tone results in airway obstruction, desaturation and rousing. This can occur 300–400 times per night, leading to daytime drowsiness, morning headaches and personality changes. Each desaturation is associated with catecholamine release resulting in surges in blood pressure. In the longer term the hypoxia may lead to an increase in pulmonary vascular resistance, pulmonary hypertension and right heart failure. Ondine's curse is not obstructive in nature but, due to a central loss of respiratory drive, results in apnoea during sleep.

Q1.52
A = True
B = False
C = False
D = True
E = True
Effective cricoid pressure is dependent upon an intact cricoid cartilage which is used to compress the oesophagus against the body of C6, thus preventing any regurgitated matter within the oesophagus from entering the pharynx and then the trachea. Complete occlusion of the oesophagus is not possible with a nasogastric tube in situ; this should be aspirated and removed prior to induction of anaesthesia. A pressure of at least 40 N and sometimes up to 64 N is necessary in order to completely occlude the oesophagus in some patients; in practice, adequate pressure is not always applied.

Q1.53
A = False
B = True
C = True
D = True
E = False
Massive transfusion can be defined as a transfusion greater than the patient's normal blood volume, or the transfusion of half the normal blood

volume per hour. Stored blood may contain up to 20 mmol litre^{-1} of potassium, thus hyperkalaemia may occur following massive transfusion. Post-transfusion alkalosis may occur as the citrate, present in stored blood to prevent it from clotting, is converted by the liver to bicarbonate. Hypocalcaemia is common, particularly if the blood transfused is cold, as hepatic function is impaired by hypothermia and citrate toxicity results in a decrease in the plasma ionised calcium levels. Dilution of platelets and clotting factors following massive transfusion results in a dilutional coagulapathy and continuing bleeding, even when the surgical source of the bleeding has been effectively treated.

Q1.54
A = False
B = False
C = True
D = True
E = True
Respiratory changes associated with ageing include an increase in functional residual capacity and residual volume. The chest wall compliance is reduced, as is the expiratory reserve volume and the vital capacity. The closing volume increases to a greater extent until it encroaches on the functional residual capacity during tidal breathing, airway collapse occurs and the A–a gradient increases. The minimal alveolar concentration of an anaesthetic agent required to provide surgical anaesthesia decreases with increasing age. The plasma volume does not vary significantly with increasing age (beyond childhood), although the intracellular and interstitial water may decrease, thus affecting the volume of distribution and the effects of anaesthetic drugs. Renal function and hepatic function both decrease markedly with ageing; this has important implications for the metabolism and clearance of anaesthetic drugs in these patients.

Q1.55
A = True
B = True
C = False
D = False
E = True
Patients who are morbidly obese, i.e. those with a body mass index greater than 35, have double the risk of developing postoperative pulmonary complications than those with a normal body mass index. The risk of postoperative pulmonary complication is also increased in patients with advanced age, a history of chest trauma, smokers, and those with pre-existing respi-

ratory disease (e.g. kyphoscoliosis, chronic obstructive pulmonary disease, haemoptysis). There is also an increased incidence of postoperative pulmonary complication following upper abdominal surgery or if postoperative pain is poorly controlled.

Q1.56
A = False
B = True
C = False
D = False
E = False

Pain during the administration of thiopentone suggests extravascular or intra-arterial injection. An anaphylactic reaction is, by definition, a Type I hypersensitivity reaction mediated by IgE. An anaphylactoid reaction may be clinically very similar or identical but is not mediated by IgE. Both reactions are more common in patients with a history of atopy (asthma, eczema, allergic rhinitis). The clinical features of an anaphylactic reaction include urticaria, bronchospasm, upper airway oedema, severe hypotension and potential cardiac arrest. The immediate management of an anaphylactic reaction is essentially supportive and must include oxygen, intravenous fluids and intramuscular adrenaline administration.

Q1.57
A = True
B = False
C = True
D = True
E = False

The incidence of awareness during general anaesthesia is approximately 1:3000. Physiological changes may easily be blocked by anaesthetic techniques such as epidural anaesthesia, with awareness present unintentionally. The isolated forearm technique has been used to evaluate awareness in volunteers. In this, a tourniquet is inflated around the upper arm to above the systolic blood pressure before the neuromuscular blocking agent is given. Arm movement (either spontaneous or in response to a command) can then be observed during anaesthesia. Patients may respond to verbal commands without postoperative recall. In clinical practice, 70% of awareness episodes are related to faulty technique, due either to equipment failure or to the administration of too low a concentration of anaesthetic gases. Correct checking of the anaesthetic machine will decrease this risk. Pain, sleep disturbance with vivid and unpleasant dreams and psychological stress can result from either conscious awareness or implicit memory. This may result in Post Traumatic Stress Syndrome.

Q1.58

A = True
B = True
C = False
D = False
E = True

Complications associated with internal jugular cannulation include puncture of the common carotid artery, pneumothorax, haemothorax, infection, damage to the brachial plexus, sympathetic chain or phrenic nerve, and damage to the thoracic duct, with left-sided line insertion. All central venous cannulation routes are associated with potential thrombus formation.

Q1.59

A = True
B = True
C = False
D = True
E = True

Absolute contraindications to epidural anaesthesia include:

i.   lack of expertise
ii.   patient refusal
iii. lack of resuscitation facilities
iv.   inability to gain vascular access
v.   local or systemic sepsis
vi.   coagulopathy
vii. known allergy to local anaesthetic agents (very rare)
viii. uncontrolled haemorrhage.

Relative contraindications to epidural anaesthesia include:

i.   neurological disease (e.g. multiple sclerosis)
ii.   potential massive haemorrhage
iii. spinal deformities
iv.   fixed cardiac output states such as severe aortic stenosis.

A thyromental distance of less than 6cm is associated with possible difficult intubation. There is a small risk of total spinal anaesthesia during epidural anaesthesia; however, this is not a contraindication to the technique as the risks of general anaesthesia may be greater.

Q1.60
A = True
B = True
C = True
D = True
E = True

Rheumatoid arthritis may be associated with laxity of the atlanto–axial ligaments, especially the transverse ligament, with erosion of the odontoid peg resulting in instability. Ankylosing spondylitis is characterised by bony ankylosis of the spine (bamboo spine). These patients are at constant risk of spinal fracture and, perhaps surprisingly, also have cervical spine instability, in particular atlanto–axial instability. Cervical metastases are the commonest cause of collapse of the cervical vertebrae which in turn may result in instability. 18% of patients with Down's syndrome have radiological evidence of atlanto–axial instability, although only 2%–3% display symptoms. Paget's disease is a metabolic disorder of unknown aetiology involving the excessively rapid remodelling of bone, which results in a susceptibility to fracture. Involvement of the cervical spine may also result in atlanto–axial instability.

Q1.61
A = False
B = False
C = True
D = False
E = False

The headache associated with raised intracranial pressure is characteristically worse in the morning and further worsened by coughing, straining and stooping. Nausea and vomiting, confusion and coma may also occur. The Cushing reflex associated with severe intracranial hypertension consists of marked hypertension and bradycardia. Diabetes insipidus, cardiac arrhythmias and loss of central temperature control may also occur. Respirations become irregular, ultimately progressing to apnoea.

Q1.62
A = True
B = True
C = True
D = False
E = True

The aspiration of gastric contents into the lungs may occur in a sedated or anaesthetised patient due to relaxation of the lower oesophageal sphincter associated with depression of the laryngeal reflexes. Conditions increasing the risk of aspiration include the presence of a full stomach, gastrointestinal obstruction such as congenital or acquired pyloric stenosis, ileus, trauma, pain, and hiatus hernia. Factors which increase intra-abdominal pressure will also increase the risk of aspiration; these include pregnancy, lithotomy postion and obesity. Also certain drugs such as atropine and the opioids may predispose to aspiration. Suxamethonium does not increase the risk; indeed it is used as part of a rapid sequence induction in patients who are at high risk of aspiration.

Q1.63
A = True
B = True
C = True
D = True
E = True

The complications associated with percutaneous tracheostomy performed in the intensive care unit are similar to those associated with conventional tracheostomy performed in the operating theatre. Complications of both techniques may be divided into immediate and late. Immediate complications include bleeding, tracheostomy malposition, tracheal perforation and upper airway obstruction, often due to herniation of the high-volume high-compliance cuff over the end of the tracheostomy tube. Late complications include infection, pneumomediastinum, tube obstruction, tracheal stenosis and bleeding. Bleeding may be particularly dramatic when it is due to the erosion of a major blood vessel such as the innominate artery, when mortality is high. If tracheo–innominate fistula is suspected the haemorrhage may be temporarily controlled by overinflating the high-volume high-compliance balloon or by inserting a finger into the tracheostomy wound anterior to the trachea and compressing the innominate artery against the sternum or clavicle. The patient may then be transferred to theatre for surgical control of the haemorrhage.

Q1.64
A = True
B = True
C = True
D = True
E = True

Autoregulation of cerebral perfusion pressure normally occurs at a mean arterial pressure of between 60 and 160 mm Hg, thus, within this range cerebral blood flow will be maintained at approximately $50\,\text{ml}\,100\,\text{g}^{-1}\,\text{min}^{-1}$ despite acute changes in arterial pressure. In patients with longstanding hypertension the range over which autoregulation occurs is raised. Injury to the brain, such as trauma, seizures or hypoxia, may result in a loss of autoregulation. All volatile anaesthetic agents impair autoregulation by causing vasodilatation. Hyperventilation resulting in hypocapnia before the administration of the volatile component may limit this effect.

Q1.65
A = False
B = False
C = True
D = True
E = True

Spinal anaesthesia is the result of local anaesthesia of the somatic and autonomic nerve fibres as they cross the subarachnoid space within the vertebral column. Preganglionic sympathetic fibres arise from the cord between T1 and L2 and synapse in the sympathetic chain, which runs on either side of the vertebral column. Blockade of these sympathetic fibres results in peripheral vasodilatation and a decrease in both systemic vascular resistance and venous return. This in turn results in a reduction in cardiac output and hypotension. The bradycardia associated with spinal anaesthesia may be due to blockade of the cardiac sympathetic fibres between T1 and T4, combined with vagal overactivity. The adrenal medulla is also supplied by preganglionic sympathetic nerve fibres that are also blocked during spinal anaesthesia, resulting in decreased levels of circulating catecholamines and a further reduction in arterial pressure. Somatic spinal nerves consist of pairs of nerves, each pair being made up of a ventral root and a dorsal root. The ventral root carries afferent motor fibres from the cord, and the dorsal root fibres carries afferent sensory fibres back to the spinal cord.

Q1.66
A = False
B = False
C = True
D = True
E = False

Dystrophia myotonica is the most common of the myotonic syndromes, occurring in around 1:20,000. It is an autosomal-dominant condition, which shows anticipation (increasing severity with each generation). The male-to-female ratio is 1:1. There are characteristic features including frontal balding, cataracts, ptosis, muscle wasting (particularly of the sternomastoid muscles, shoulder muscles and quadriceps). The disease is associated with a low IQ, gonadal atrophy, diabetes mellitus, respiratory failure due to muscle weakness, poor central control of respiration and obstructive sleep apnoea, cardiac conduction defects and cardiomyopathy and delayed gastric emptying. Thyroid and adrenal impairment may also be present. Patients usually present between 20 and 40 years of age and die in their 60s. Myotonia (delayed muscle relaxation following muscle contraction) may be precipitated by suxamethonium, cold, shivering, hypokalaemia and neostigmine and may render laryngoscopy and tracheal intubation difficult or impossible.

Q1.67
A = False
B = True
C = False
D = True
E = False
Clinical signs, which indicate adequate reversal of neuromuscular blockade, include an ability to open the eyes widely, stick out the tongue, cough effectively, maintain a sustained hand grip and raise the head off the pillow for at least 5 seconds. These clinical features correlate with a train-of-four ratio of 0.75. If the patient cannot lift their head off the pillow for 5 seconds, it is likely that there is still a significant residual reduction in vital capacity and inspiratory force. The ability to maintain arterial oxygenation saturation while supplemental oxygen is being delivered does not confirm the adequacy of ventilation, as inadequate tidal ventilation may prevent desaturation while the arterial carbon dioxide tension progressively rises.

Q1.68
A = False
B = False
C = False
D = False
E = True
Pyloric stenosis occurs in approximately 1:1500 live births and approximately 80% of affected infants are male. The babies characteristically present at around four to six weeks of age with projectile vomiting and a failure to gain weight. Following a feed, a mass may be palpable in the epigastrium or right hypochondrium. There may be severe hypovolaemia associated with a hypochloraemic hypokalaemic alkalosis. Preoperative management should include gastric drainage via a nasogastric tube, rehydration and correction of the metabolic disturbance. The infant should not undergo surgery until the serum sodium is greater than 135 mmol litre^{-1}, the chloride greater than 90 mmol litre^{-1} and the bicarbonate is 24–30 mmol litre^{-1}.

Q1.69
A = False
B = False
C = False
D = False
E = False

Acute epiglottitis usually occurs in children between the ages of 2 and 5 years, but it may also occur in adults, usually between 20 and 40 years. It is caused in over 50% of cases by the Haemophilus influenzae virus type B. The incidence of epiglottitis in the UK has fallen since the introduction of the HiB vaccine. If the diagnosis of acute epiglottis is suspected, the child and parent are moved without delay or upset to the anaesthetic room in order to allow tracheal intubation under anaesthesia. Performing a neck x-ray, taking a throat swab or inserting an intravenous cannula while the child is still awake is absolutely contraindicated. Orotracheal intubation should be performed following an inhalational induction by an experienced anaesthetist with an ENT surgeon standing by. The oral endotracheal tube is then often exchanged for a nasal one, as this is generally better tolerated by the child. However, this is not mandatory, particularly if the intubation was difficult.

Q1.70
A = True
B = True
C = False
D = False
E = True

Normal pregnancy may be associated with glycosuria due to a reduction in the tubular resorption of glucose. Fanconi's syndrome is the result of defective tubular resorption of most amino acids, glucose, phosphate and bicarbonate. Conversely the glycosuria associated with a phaeochromocytoma is due to the increased circulating levels of catecholamines suppressing insulin release, thus leading to hyperglycaemia. Zollinger–Ellison syndrome is due to a tumour which produces very high plasma gastrin levels which, in turn, result in gastric acid hypersecretion and recurrent duodenal ulceration. The tumour is usually benign and glycosuria does not occur. Carcinoid syndrome is due to a metastatic tumour secreting 5-hydroxytryptamine; again this is not usually associated with glycosuria.

Q1.71

A = True
B = True
C = True
D = True
E = False

In patients undergoing coronary bypass grafting, certain patient characteristics are associated with an increased risk of perioperative morbidity or mortality. These include myocardial infarction within the preceding six months, congestive cardiac failure as evidenced by a gallop rhythm, associated valvular disease and advanced age (particularly greater than 80 years). Chronic stable angina and left main stem disease do not in themselves confer increased risk, although it is clearly important to be aware of their presence as this will influence the subsequent management of the patient. Other significant risk factors include diabetes, hypertension, obesity, renal or hepatic impairment.

Q1.72

A = False
B = False
C = True
D = False
E = True

Statistics is the mathematical treatment of experimentally obtained observations. Nominal data are placed into categories without numerical value (e.g. male/female). Ordinal data (data which can be ranked numerically) from clinical trials is described as parametric (normal distribution) or non-parametric. The central tendency (mean, mode, median) and scatter (standard deviation and percentiles) are used to describe the histogram representations of ordinal data. The appropriate statistical test will give a result as the probability of any difference between two groups being due to chance (the null hypothesis). A significant result is conventionally accepted as $P < 0.05$. Ordinal non-parametric data is described by the median and percentiles; normally distributed data by the mean and standard deviation. Student's *t*-test is used to compare the mean and standard deviation between groups of normally distributed parametric data. A Type II error is a false negative.

Type 1 = False positive

Q1.73
A = False
B = True
C = False
D = False
E = True

Audit is part of the Clinical Governance agenda and effective audit is crucial to the development of good practice. It may be defined as the systematic critical analysis of the procedures for diagnosis, care and treatment, and includes examining the use of resources and analysis of outcomes. The audit cycle includes: developing an audit question, investigating present practice, making changes and then re-auditing to assess the effect of the intervention. The Royal College of Anaesthetists has issued an audit recipe book, 'Raising the Standard', with suggestions of useful audits for all departments. Audit data does not need to be statistically analysed to provide useful information. Benchmarking is related to comparing data, e.g. the use of day-care services in different trusts both doing the same type of surgical work.

Q1.74
A = False
B = True
C = True
D = True
E = False

The Serious Hazards of Transfusion (SHOT) Scheme was started in 1996 and aimed to collect data on serious sequelae of transfusion of blood components, including:
i.   incorrect blood component transfused (even if no harm arises)
ii.   acute or delayed transfusion reactions
iii. transfusion-related graft-versus-host disease
iv.   transfusion-related lung injury
v.   post-transfusion purpura
vi.   autologous predeposit incidents
vii. bacterial contamination
viii. post-transfusion viral infection.

Cases must be reported in the first instance to the hospital haematologist who relays the information to the SHOT Coordinator. An annual report is then produced and publicised in order to facilitate the development of strategies aimed at the prevention and treatment of these complications.

Q1.75
A = True
B = True
C = True
D = True
E = True

Latex allergy may be characterised by urticaria, rhinitis, conjunctivitis, dyspnoea and systemic reactions including anaphylaxis. High-risk groups include healthcare workers, patients with urogenital abnormalities and, less frequently, patients attending allergy clinics. History-taking should include the precise timing of the reaction, the presence of sneezing, rhinorrhoea, pruritis or urticaria after contact with rubber articles. There may be associated fruit allergies, most commonly to banana, avocado or chestnut. Skin prick testing and immunoassay may confirm a suspected diagnosis of latex allergy. Although there is clearly a spectrum of sensitivity, it is safest to advise avoidance of contact with latex as far as is possible. High-risk patients should be treated in a latex-free environment. All patients with latex allergy should consider wearing a MedicAlert bracelet, and those who have suffered a life-threatening reaction should carry an Epipen.

Q1.76
A = True
B = True
C = True
D = True
E = True

If the central venous catheter, as visualised on the post-procedure chest x-ray, is seen to take an unusual course, it may indicate that the catheter is either extravascular, arterial, or within a smaller vein such as the internal thoracic or left superior intercostal vein. Other complications of central venous cannulation visible on the chest x-ray include pneumothorax, venous or arterial perforation with extrapleural, pleural or mediastinal haemorrhage, ectopic infusion, cardiac perforation, retained wire, air embolism or a knotted catheter.

Q1.77
A = True
B = False
C = False
D = False
E = True

Myxodema coma may occur in a patient with hypothyroidism who is subjected to an external stress, e.g. infection, trauma, hypothermia or surgery.

It is characterised by confusion and psychosis, progressing to coma. Bradycardia, pericardial effusion, ileus, megacolon, hypothermia, anaemia and respiratory failure may all be present. Seizures, hyperpyrexia and tachycardia are signs of thyrotoxic crisis, not myxodema coma. Myxodema coma is a medical emergency with a high mortality and therefore management should include admission to the intensive care unit, maintenance of normovolaemia, passive re-warming, ventilatory support as necessary and the intravenous administration of thyroxine.

2. Applied Anatomy

Q2.1 The carina in an adult is:

A. at the level of the xiphisternum
B. approximately 10 cm from the cricoid cartilage
C. about 2.5 cm from the right upper lobe bronchus
D. at post mortem at the level of T4
E. above the level of the arch of the aorta

Q2.2 The vagus nerve:

A. supplies motor fibres to all the muscles of the larynx
B. descends in the neck within the carotid sheath
C. on the right gives off its recurrent laryngeal branch at the lower border of the aortic arch and therefore may be damaged during ligation of a patent ductus arteriosus
D. supplies sensory fibres to the dura mater
E. supplies all the intrinsic and extrinsic muscles of the tongue

Q2.3 In relation to the first rib:

A. scalenus medius inserts into the scalene tubercle
B. the lower trunk of the brachial plexus lies on the lower surface
C. the subclavian artery lies in front of the scalene tubercle
D. the superior intercostal artery lies anterior to its neck
E. it articulates solely with T1

Q2.4 The following statements are true:

A. the coronary sinus drains into the right atrium of the heart
B. in 70% of patients the sinoatrial node is supplied by a branch of the left coronary artery
C. on a lateral x-ray of the chest, the left ventricle lies anterior to the right ventricle
D. on a posterior–anterior x-ray of the chest, the right ventricle forms the inferior border of the heart
E. closure of the ductus arteriosus is triggered soon after birth by the rise in the circulating oxygen tension.

Q2.5 In relation to a caudal block:

A. it is a subdural injection through the sacrococcygeal ligament
B. piercing the dural sac may occur as it usually extends to the upper border of the fifth lumbar vertebra
C. it is associated with some parasympathetic blockade
D. the volume of the caudal space is remarkably constant in the adult
E. it should be avoided in obstetric practice

Q2.6 Blockade of the trigeminal ganglion with local anaesthetic:

A. may be performed percutaneously
B. is associated with anaesthesia of the angle of the mandible
C. is associated with anaesthesia of the soft palate
D. is first-line treatment of trigeminal neuralgia
E. is usually performed under image intensification

Q2.7 The epidural space:

A. extends from the foramen magnum to the sacrococcygeal membrane
B. contains nerve roots, blood vessels, lymphatics and fat
C. is widest in the cervical and lumbar regions
D. the distance between the ligamentum flava and the dura may be less that 2mm in the lumbar region
E. is more easily accessed with a lower incidence of dural puncture via the paramedian approach rather than the mid-line approach

Q2.8 A coeliac plexus block:

A. may relieve visceral abdominal pain
B. may relieve the pain of chronic pancreatitis
C. may be complicated by impotence
D. should only be performed unilaterally to avoid severe hypotension
E. blocks sympathetic and parasympathetic fibres

Q2.9 With reference to the brachial plexus:

A. as it passes over the first rib, the brachial plexus lies immediately anterior to the subclavian artery
B. the injection of local anaesthetic via the axillary approach may be complicated by inadvertent intra-arterial injection
C. the phrenic nerve is a branch of the upper trunk
D. the roots may be blocked with an interscalene block between medius and scalenus posterior
E. the divisions are formed at the lateral border of the first rib

Q2.10 The ductus arteriosus:

A. is a communication between the ascending aorta and the left pulmonary artery
B. usually closes within 48 hours of birth
C. closes when the PaO_2 rises
D. may be patent in good health
E. if it remains patent it results in a right-to-left shunt

Q2.11 The following statements are true with regard to the use of local anaesthetic blocks in the foot:

A. in order to anaesthetise the foot completely it is necessary to block all five nerves supplying it
B. the saphenous nerve may be blocked at the level of the lateral malleolus
C. arterial injection may complicate a tibial nerve block
D. contrary to digital blocks in the hand, adrenaline is not contraindicated when performing a digital block in the foot
E. sensation to the dorsum of the foot is entirely supplied by the superficial peroneal nerve

Q2.12 The pressure in the lumbar epidural space:

A. is always subatmospheric
B. varies with intrathoracic pressure
C. may be positive in patients with severe chronic obstructive airways disease
D. must be negative when the 'hanging drop' method is used to detect the space
E. is influenced by the presence of a Tuohy needle in the space

Q2.13 The following statements are true:

A. the ulnar artery is larger than the radial artery
B. the lingual lobe of the left lung has two segments
C. sensation to the anterior two-thirds of the tongue is supplied by the lingual nerve
D. the common peroneal nerve is one of the two terminal branches of the sciatic nerve
E. the intercostal nerves travel between the external and internal intercostal muscles

Q2.14 In relation to the diaphragm:

A. the oesophagus traverses it at the level of T8
B. the dome of the right hemidiaphragm reaches the level of the fifth rib in the midclavicular line
C. congenital hernia is most common on the left
D. the right hemidiaphragm is higher than the left due to the presence of the liver
E. the left crus is larger than the right

Q2.15 The lumbar plexus:

A. is formed by the posterior primary rami of the lumbar roots 1–4
B. includes the sciatic nerve
C. forms the main sensory nerve supply to the hip
D. may be completely blocked by a small volume of local anaesthetic solution at the level of the third lumbar vertebra
E. supplies sensation to the skin over the lateral aspect of the thigh

Answers to Section 2

Q2.1
A = False
B = False
C = True
D = True
E = False

The carina in the cadaver is at the level of T4 (manubriosternal junction, or Angle of Louis) and is approximately 15 cm below the cricoid cartilage. The right main bronchus is shorter and wider than the left and the right upper lobe bronchus originates 2.5 cm from the carina. The aorta arches over the left main bronchus and therefore is above the level of the carina.

Q2.2
A = True
B = True
C = False
D = True
E = False

The vagus nerve provides all the motor supply to the laryngeal muscles via its recurrent laryngeal and superior laryngeal branches, in addition to supplying the bronchial muscles, respiratory tract, gut, heart, dura and epiglottis. It descends in the neck between the internal jugular vein and the common carotid artery within the carotid sheath. Within the thorax the right vagus nerve gives off its recurrent laryngeal nerve at the lower border of the subclavian artery and the left vagus nerve gives off its recurrent laryngeal branch at the lower level of the aortic arch. The left recurrent laryngeal nerve then loops around the aortic arch close to the ligamentum arteriosum before ascending in the mediastinum into the neck. This prolonged intrathoracic course renders the left recurrent laryngeal nerve prone to injury during patent ductus arteriosus ligation or dissection around the hilum of the left lung. The hypoglossal nerve supplies all of the intrinsic and extrinsic muscles of the tongue.

Q2.3
A = False
B = False
C = False
D = True
E = True

The first rib bears on its inner margin the scalene tubercle (tubercle of Lisfranc) to which scalenus anterior inserts. The first rib has a rounded head bearing a single facet which articulates with the body of the first thoracic vertebra. Crossing the neck of the first rib are the sympathetic trunk, a branch of the anterior primary ramus of the first thoracic nerve, the superior intercostal artery and vein. Superiorly its relations include the subclavian artery which lies behind the scalene tubercle, and the lower trunk of the brachial plexus.

Q2.4
A = True
B = False
C = False
D = True
E = True

The coronary sinus provides the majority of the venous drainage of the heart and drains into the right atrium close to the origin of the inferior vena cava. The remaining venous drainage of the heart is provided by the thebesian veins which drain directly into the right atrium. The sinoatrial node is supplied by a branch of the right coronary artery. The right atrium and ventricle lie anterior to the left atrium and ventricle on a lateral chest x-ray. On a posterior–anterior x-ray of the chest the right atrium makes up the right heart border, the right ventricle makes up the inferior border and the left ventricle forms the left heart border. The left atrium is situated posteriorly. The ductus arteriosus is a part of the foetal circulation connecting the aorta and the pulmonary artery. This allows blood in utero to shunt directly from the pulmonary artery into the systemic circulation, thus bypassing the pulmonary vascular bed (right-to-left shunt). The duct normally closes within a few days of birth, triggered by a rise in arterial oxygen tension. If this does not occur a significant left-to-right shunt may develop, eventually resulting in irreversible pulmonary hypertension. A persistant ductus arteriosus may be closed either surgically or with a device introduced via a catheter during cardiac catheterisation.

Q2.5
A = False
B = False
C = True
D = False
E = False

The dural and arachnoid sacs in the adult usually terminate at the level of the second sacral vertebra; in an infant they may extend to the level of the third or fourth sacral vertebrae, below which is the caudal space, thus a caudal block is an extradural injection. Access to this space is gained through the sacrococcygeal ligament or membrane. In adults there is considerable anatomical variation in the size and shape of the sacral hiatus and the volume of the caudal space may vary between 10 and 25 ml. As the sacral component of the parasympathetic nervous system is carried in the anterior primary rami of S2, 3 and 4, these will be blocked as they traverse the caudal space. Caudal analgesia has long been used in obstetric practice and did in fact historically precede the use of lumbar epidural analgesia in the quest for painless labour.

Q2.6
A = True
B = False
C = True
D = False
E = True

The trigeminal nerve is the largest cranial nerve. It supplies sensation to the face, excluding the angle of the mandible, most of the scalp, the teeth, mouth, and nasal cavity. It also has a small motor component which provides innervation to the muscles of mastication. Trigeminal neuralgia is characterised by intermittent exquisite pain in the territory of the trigeminal nerve, usually the mandibular division. Medical management may include traditional analgesics, carbamazepine, phenytoin and clonazepam. If this is ineffective surgical decompression of the trigeminal nerve may be performed or the nerve may be destroyed by the injection of alcohol, usually via a percutaneous approach with image intensification.

Q2.7
A = True
B = True
C = True
D = True
E = True

The epidural space extends from the foramen magnum to the sacrococcygeal membrane. It is bounded internally by the dura and arachnoid mater and externally by the posterior longitudinal ligament, the ligamentum flavum, the intervertebral foramina and the vertebral pedicles. It may extend through the intervertebral foramina into the paravertebral space. The epidural space may be located between 2 and 9 cm from the skin in a normal adult.

Q2.8
A = True
B = True
C = True
D = False
E = True
The coeliac plexus lies anterior to the aorta at the level of the first lumbar vertebra. Coeliac plexus block is one of the most effective methods of controlling visceral pain; in particular it is often used to control the pain associated with pancreatic and gastric tumours and chronic pancreatitis. The plexus contains both visceral afferent and efferent sympathetic fibres and preganglionic parasympathetic fibres. The block is necessarily bilateral in order to provide adequate pain relief due to crossover of fibres. Complications include hypotension, which may be severe even after unilateral block, intravascular injection, intrathecal injection, impaired hip flexion and impotence.

Q2.9
A = False
B = True
C = False
D = False
E = True
The brachial plexus is formed by the anterior primary rami of C5–T1. It supplies the majority of the innervation to the upper limb, except for the intercostobrachial and brachial cutaneous nerves which are derived from T2. It has five roots lying between scalenus medius and scalenus anterior. As it passes over the first rib, the brachial plexus lies immediately behind the subclavian artery and divides into three trunks (upper, middle and lower). Below the clavicle the brachial plexus surrounds the axillary artery as the medial, lateral and posterior cords. The cords are closely related to the axillary artery within a neurovascular sheath, thus injection of local anaesthetic at this level may be complicated by intra-arterial injection. The interscalene block is the most proximal approach to the brachial plexus and involves injection of local anaesthetic into the groove between scalenus medius and

scalenus anterior at the level of the cricoid cartilage. The external jugular vein often crosses the groove at this point The phrenic nerve is derived mainly from C4, with contributions from C3 and C5.

Q2.10
A = False
B = True
C = True
D = True
E = False

The ductus arteriosus is a communication between the pulmonary trunk and the descending aorta. At birth the rise in PaO_2 and fall in hydrogen ion concentration produce contraction of the wall of the ductus resulting in functional closure. In the course of the next 2–3 months it becomes completely obliterated. A patent ductus arteriosus is relatively common and may be present for many years without symptoms. However, if not corrected the left-to-right shunt ultimately will result in progressive left ventricular hypertrophy and pulmonary hypertension

Q2.11
A = True
B = False
C = True
D = False
E = False

In order to anaesthetise a foot completely using an ankle block, all five nerves supplying the foot must be blocked. These comprise the saphenous, sural, superficial peroneal, deep peroneal and the tibial nerves. The saphenous nerve is closely associated with the long saphenous vein and therefore may be blocked at the level of the medial maleolus. The saphenous nerve may be damaged during harvesting of the long saphenous vein for coronary artery surgery, with resultant numbness along the medial border of the foot and medial aspect of the arch of the sole. The deep peroneal and tibial nerves may be blocked close to dorsalis pedis and the posterior tibial artery respectively, thus these blocks may potentially be complicated by intra-arterial injection. Digital blocks may be performed in the foot in the same way as in the hand. The use of adrenaline-containing solutions is absolutely contraindicated; in addition, these blocks should be avoided in patients with peripheral vascular disease.

Q2.12
A = False
B = True
C = True
D = True
E = False

There is communication between the epidural space and the paravertebral space. In the thorax the paravertebral space is only separated from the pleural cavity by the parietal pleura. Pressure changes in the pleural cavity are therefore transmitted via the paravertebral space to the epidural space. Deep inspiration will generate a negative extradural pressure, whereas coughing will generate a positive pressure; indeed in patients with chronic obstructive airways disease the pressure may be predominantly positive. The hanging drop method of identifying the epidural space depends on the presence of a negative pressure, therefore it can bee seen that this is not a reliable method for identifying the epidural space. The pressure is not influenced by the presence of a Tuohy needle in the space.

Q2.13
A = True
B = True
C = True
D = True
E = False

The lingual lobe has a superior and an inferior segment. The intercostal nerves travel with the intercostal arteries and veins between the internal and innermost intercostal muscles in a groove along the lower border of the corresponding rib. The sciatic nerve ends at the level of the popliteal fossa, dividing into the tibial and common peroneal nerves. The tibial nerve descends in the flexor compartment of the leg to the medial malleolus, where it divides into the medial and lateral popliteal nerves. The common peroneal nerve descends through the popliteal fossa and divides into the superficial and deep peroneal nerves. Sensation to the anterior two-thirds of the tongue is supplied by the lingual nerve, which is a branch of the mandibular division of the trigeminal nerve. Sensation to the posterior third of the tongue is supplied by the glossopharyngeal nerve.

Q2.14
A = False
B = True
C = True
D = True
E = False

The oesophagus traverses the diaphragm at the level of T10, the inferior vena cava at T8 and the aorta, thoracic duct and azygos vein at T12. The right hemidiaphragm is higher than the left because of the pressure of the liver. The crura arise from the lumbar vertebral bodies, the left from L1 and L2 and the larger right from L1, L2 and L3.

Q2.15
A = False
B = False
C = True
D = False
E = True

The lumbar plexus is formed by the anterior primary rami of the first to the fourth lumbar nerve roots as they pass through the psoas muscle. The nerves formed include the iliohypogastric, ilioinguinal, genitofemoral, lateral cutaneous nerve of the thigh, obturator and femoral. The sciatic nerve is formed from the lumbosacral trunk, part of the sacral plexus. Sensation to the hip is provided by the lumbar plexus plus a small contribution from the subcostal nerve (T12); sensation to the lateral aspect of the thigh is provided by the lateral cutaneous nerve of the thigh. A lumbar plexus block may be achieved by injecting a large volume of local anaesthetic solution (30–50ml) deep to the transverse process of the third lumbar vertebra, a smaller-volume block may be used to supplement general anaesthesia.

3. Applied Physiology

Q3.1 In the following genetic conditions:

A. the gene for malignant hyperpyrexia is located on chromosome 19
B. the gene for central core disease is located on chromosome 19
C. the most useful test for screening for MH-susceptible patients is DNA analysis
D. patients with C1 esterase deficiency have a prolonged paralysis following suxamethonium
E. patients with Duchenne's Muscular Dystrophy have low cholinesterase levels and suxamethonium use is contraindicated

Q3.2 The secretion of gastric acid:

A. is stimulated by gastrin
B. is inhibited by histamine
C. is from the parietal cells of the gastric mucosa
D. inhibits gastrin secretion
E. is inhibited by secretin

Q3.3 The following statements are true with respect to the physiological changes associated with drug abuse:

A. cocaine users may have increased noradrenaline levels.
B. amphetamine use is associated with decreased CNS catecholamine levels
C. the majority of intravenous drug abusers have abnormal liver function
D. patients addicted to opiates often have an increased CO_2 drive to respiration
E. postoperative opiates should be avoided in known opiate addicts

Q3.4 When considering pituitary function:

A. prolactin secretion is inhibited by the secretion of dopamine from the hypothalamus
B. growth hormone, luteinising hormone and follicular stimulating hormone are secreted by the anterior pituitary
C. Anti-diuretic hormone (ADH) release from the posterior pituitary is independent of hypothalamic control
D. insufficient ADH production results in the polydipsia and polyuria of diabetes mellitus
E. following anterior pituitary failure, corticosteroids are required perioperatively

Q3.5 In the elderly patient:

A. dysrhythmias are more common because of decreased numbers of sino-atrial node pacemaker cells
B. increasing cardiac output is achieved mainly by increasing stroke volume
C. plasma catecholamine levels are higher and this causes an increased incidence of hypertension
D. the glomerular filtration rate decreases exponentially with age
E. poor temperature control may result in postoperative hypothermia.

Q3.6 In the young adult:

A. anorexia may be the diagnosis if the person perceives they are overweight yet their actual weight is 15% below predicted for their age.
B. anorexics tend to have a resting tachycardia
C. in anorexia the stomach is usually empty
D. genetic factors are the most important determinant of an adult's weight
E. a body mass index of 24 is considered normal

Q3.7 Altitude sickness:

A. may be treated with intravenous acetaminophen
B. occurs approximately one week after ascent to high altitude
C. acclimatisation involves an increase in 2,3-DPG levels
D. treatment includes rest and acetazolamide
E. may be associated with acute pulmonary oedema

Q3.8 The following statements are true of the healthy adult:

A. the functional residual capacity may be the same as the residual volume
B. the vital capacity is the sum of the expiratory and inspiratory reserve volumes
C. the normal residual volume is about 600ml
D. functional residual capacity may be measured by helium dilution
E. the anatomical dead space may be deduced from the nitrogen washout

Q3.9 Pain sensation:

A. acute pain is transmitted via fast Aδ fibres which terminate in the lamina I in the spinal cord
B. pain is transmitted via slower myelinated C fibres
C. opioid receptors occur in the dorsal horn
D. most descending pathways have an inhibitory effect on pain sensation
E. polymodal nocioceptors transmit pain associated with pinprick and heat

Q3.10 With regard to the neuromuscular junction:

A. it includes both presynaptic and postsynaptic areas
B. the junctional folds contain high concentrations of pseudocholinesterase
C. the nicotinic acetylcholine receptor consists of five sub units.
D. acetylcholine is inactivated by passing through the calcium channels
E. the presynaptic release of acetylcholine is calcium mediated

Q3.11 The carotid bodies:

A. have less blood flow per gram of tissue than brain
B. respond to a decrease in pH
C. respond to a decrease in blood pressure
D. are situated in the arch of the aorta
E. are innervated by the vagus nerve

Q3.12 Causes of giant 'a' waves (cannon waves) in the jugular venous pulse include:

A. aortic incompetence
B. a nodal or junctional rhythm
C. pulmonary hypertension
D. complete heart block
E. pulmonary stenosis

Q3.13 In a previously healthy adult subjected to starvation:

A. there is an increase in insulin production
B. ketosis is common
C. breakdown of protein from the muscles, liver and spleen occurs
D. death will occur in approximately 20 days of no food intake
E. T3 levels decrease

Q3.14 With regard to calcium homeostasis:

A. release of parathyroid hormone is stimulated by hypocalcaemia and hypermagnesaemia
B. hypocalcaemia may result in tetany
C. in pseudohypoparathyroidism, circulating PTH levels are decreased
D. in secondary hyperparathyroidism, the kidneys do not respond to the high levels of 1,25 dihydroxycholecalciferol
E. calcitonin is secreted by the parathyroids and results in a lowering of the plasma calcium levels

Q3.15 When considering the sympathetic and parasympathetic systems:

A. dopamine is a transmitter at the sympathetic nerve ending
B. clonidine stimulates at the α2 receptors
C. bretilyum blocks adrenaline release at the postganglionic norepinephric neurone
D. coronary vasoconstriction is effected via α1 receptor activity
E. sacral parasympathetic outflow is via S234 spinal nerves

Q3.16 In the normal adult:

A. blood flow decreases during the active phase of muscle contraction
B. the cardiac output can increase above 20 litres min^{-1} during exercise
C. athletes have a larger stroke volume and higher heart rate than non-athletes
D. the percentage of blood flow that goes to the brain is little changed during exercise
E. blood flow to exercising muscle is decreased by a decrease in tissue PO_2 and an increase in PCO_{65}

Q3.17 With regard to antidiuretic hormone (ADH):

A. it is a polypeptide
B. secretion is increased during exercise
C. it acts at the descending limb of the loop of Henle
D. decreased plasma osmolality stimulates secretion
E. deficiency may present as polyuria and polydipsia

Q3.18 With regard to the oxygen dissociation curve:

A. a rise in pH due to hyperventilation will shift the curve to the right
B. HbF has a greater affinity for oxygen than HbA2
C. hypothermia shifts the curve to the right
D. ascent to high altitude decreases 2,3-DPG levels and therefore shifts the curve to the right
E. hyperkalaemia shifts the curve to the left

Q3.19 In the normal lung in the erect position:

A. blood flow is greatest at the base
B. ventilation is greatest at the apex
C. the alveolar partial pressure of carbon dioxide (P_ACO_2) is greatest at the apex
D. at the base of the lung the blood flow is dependent on the arteriovenous pressure difference
E. hypotension results in an increase in the physiological dead space.

Q3.20 The physiological responses to hypoxia include:

A. tachycardia
B. pulmonary vasoconstriction
C. increased systemic vascular resistance
D. cerebral vasodilatation
E. increased circulating catecholamines

Q3.21 Blood flow through the coronary arteries:

A. predominately occurs in diastole
B. is about $100 \, ml \, min^{-1}$ in the adult
C. is reduced during a tachycardia
D. is influenced by local metabolism
E. is decreased by an increase in venous pressure

Q3.22 Acetylcholine is the neurotransmitter at:

A. sympathetic nerve terminals supplying the heart
B. sympathetic nerve terminals in the adrenal medulla
C. parasympathetic nerve terminals supplying the lacrimal glands
D. sympathetic nerve terminals supplying sweat glands
E. sympathetic ganglia

Q3.23 With regard to thyroid function:

A. thyroxine is highly protein-bound
B. thyroxine is a glycoprotein
C. thyroxine (T4) is more potent than triiodothyronine (T3)
D. thyroid hormones act to increase the metabolic rate
E. due to negative feedback, plasma thyroid stimulating hormone(TSH)
   levels are inversely related to the free T4 level

Q3.24 Erythropoietin production is:

A. stimulated by hypercarbia
B. stimulated by hypoxia
C. increased in liver disease
D. reduced in renal disease
E. inhibited by theophylline

Q3.25 The hormone glucagon:

A. has its release triggered by high levels of plasma glucose
B. is opposed by insulin
C. is a positive inotrope
D. causes gastric acid secretion
E. is a neurotransmitter

Q3.26 The following statements are true of muscle fibres:

A. each skeletal muscle fibre is a single multinucleated cell
B. both contraction and relaxation are active processes
C. smooth muscle fibres are striated
D. cardiac muscle fibres are joined by intercalated discs
E. the endoplasmic reticulum stores calcium essential for muscular
   contraction

Q3.27 A serum potassium of 6.2 mmol litre⁻¹ and a serum sodium of 120 mmol litre⁻¹ may be associated with:

A. Addison's disease
B. Cushing's disease
C. Conn's syndrome
D. hypopituitarism
E. acute renal failure

Q3.28 The following statements are true:

A. the taste buds are situated on the filiform papillae
F. the reticular activating system controls consciousness
C. gamma aminobutyric acid is an inhibitory neurotransmitter
D. angiotensin II is one of the most potent vasodilators known
E. cerebrospinal fluid is secreted by the choroid plexus and resorbed by the arachnoid villi

Q3.29 The adrenal gland produces:

A. noradrenaline from the cortex
B. oestrogens from the medulla
C. progesterone from the medulla
D. aldosterone from the zona glomerulosa
E. glucocorticoids from the cortex

Q3.30 When considering the results of haematological investigations:

A. foetal haemoglobin levels are raised in thalassaemia
B. the normal neonate has 5%–10% foetal haemoglobin
C. a haemoglobin level of 19 g dl⁻¹ may be normal if the patient lives at altitude.
D. sickle cell trait is present if the sickle haemoglobin is greater than 70%
E. the anaemia following acute blood loss is normochromic and microcytic

Answers to Section 3

Q3.1
A = True
B = True
C = False
D = False
E = False

The gene for MH has been charted at 12–13q location on chromosome 19 and the gene for central core disease is also on this chromosome. Central core disease is clinically linked to MH susceptibility. Although the MH gene is identified, it is not consistently found in all affected patients, so other locations may be found and DNA screening is not a practical screening test at present.

C1 esterase deficiency produces the condition of hereditary angioneurotic oedema. This is an autosomal-dominant condition resulting in episodes of widespread oedema sometimes provoked by surgery, particularly dental surgery. There is no connection with pseudocholinesterase deficiency. Similarly Duchenne's is not linked to abnormal cholinesterase levels and suxamethonium is contraindicated because the hyperkalaemia resulting from abnormal muscle response to this drug may result in dysrrhythmias and cardiac arrest in these patients.

Q3.2
A = True
B = False
C = True
D = True
E = True

The secretion of acid by the parietal cells of the stomach is stimulated by gastrin, histamine (acting at H_2 receptors) and acetylcholine acting at M_3 receptors. These increase the active transport of hydrogen ions into the gastric lumen by H^+/K^+ ATPase. The decrease in intraluminal pH feeds back to inhibit further gastrin secretion, as does the hormone secretin, which is secreted by the S cells of the small intestine, and whose main action is the production of watery alkaline pancreatic juices. Gastrin secretion by the G cells of the gastric antrum is affected by the presence of stomach contents, stimulation of the vagus and blood levels of calcium and adrenaline.

Q3.3
A = True
B = False
C = True
D = False
E = False

In cocaine users the increased noradrenaline levels are caused by decreased re-uptake following cocaine use. Catecholamine levels are increased centrally in patients who use amphetamines. Both may result in increased anaesthetic requirements. Up to 70% of intravenous drug abusers will be HbsAg positive and many will, in addition, have hepatitis C or A. Abnormal liver function may also result from drug-induced hepatitis, and alcoholic liver disease is frequently present too. The pulmonary effects are various, but opiate abuse may result in a decreased respiratory response to increases in $PaCO_2$ and potential respiratory depression. Chronic interstitial lung changes can occur due to the carrier agent used with some inhaled drugs (cornstarch or talc), and this may further compromise respiratory function. Analgesic regimes must be tailored to the type of surgery and the patient. Addicts may require increased doses of opiates postoperatively and those on regular methadone will usually take that as well. Drugs which act as partial agonists at opiate receptors such as buprenorphine should be avoided as they may cause acute withdrawal syndrome. Local anaesthetic techniques can be very useful in this group of patients.

Q3.4
A = True
B = True
C = False
D = False
E = True

The anterior pituitary secretes thyroid stimulating hormone, adrenocorticotrophic hormone, luteinising hormone (LH), follicle stimulating hormone (FSH), prolactin, growth hormone and melanin-secreting hormone. Their release is controlled by the hypothalamus and specific releasing factors such as thyrotrophin-releasing factor for TSH, corticotrophin-releasing factor for adrenocorticotrophic hormone (ACTH), luteinising hormone-releasing factor for LH and FSH. Somatostatin from the hypothalamus controls growth hormone by inhibiting its release, and dopamine inhibits the release of prolactin. ACTH-dependent Cushing's syndrome results from an excess of corticosteroid, usually due to a basophilic adenoma in the anterior pituitary. Acromegaly results from excess growth hormone in the adult, due to an eosinophilic adenoma of the anterior pituitary.

The posterior pituitary secretes oxytocin and antidiuretic hormone. Inadequate production of ADH by the posterior pituitary results in diabetes insipidus and occurs most frequently following cerebral trauma, pituitary tumours and post-hypophysectomy. Secretion of ADH is controlled by plasma osmolality acting via osmoreceptors in the hypothalamus and also by changes in blood volume and blood pressure acting via baroreceptors.

Exogenous steroid replacement will be required for life in the event of anterior pituitary failure.

Q3.5
A = True
B = True
C = False
D = False
E = True

The number of sino-atrial node pacemaker cells decreases with age and at 80 years of age up to 75% have been lost, thus increasing the incidence of arrhythmias. As elderly patients have reduced ventricular compliance and a relatively lower maximum heart rate, the major contributing factor to increasing the cardiac output is an increase in stroke volume by increasing the end diastolic volume.

Ageing results in decreased compliance of blood vessels and systolic hypertension is common. There is ventricular hypertrophy, myocardial fibrosis and increasing tendency towards the development of valvular heart disease. The elderly therefore tolerate rapid fluid changes poorly. Silent myocardial infarction is common, particularly on the 3rd–4th day post-operatively. Catecholamine levels are increased; however, this is balanced by a decreased sensitivity of the end organ receptors and a clinical effect is not apparent.

The glomerular filtration rate declines above the age of 40 at approximately the rate of $1 \, \mathrm{ml \, min^{-1}}$ per year. The elderly are therefore at increased risk of acute renal failure, particularly postoperatively, and additional care must be taken with fluid replacement and drug regimes. One of the most common associations with acute renal failure in this group is the use of NSAIDs in the volume-depleted patient.

The elderly show a decreasing ability to maintain their body temperature, particularly when they are poorly nourished. They may have decreased body mass and their central control mechanisms are less effective. Peripheral perfusion is frequently compromised by peripheral vascular disease. These factors contribute to difficulties in temperature control, particularly in the postoperative period.

Q3.6

A = True
B = False
C = False
D = True
E = True

If a person perceives that they are overweight yet their actual weight is 15% below predicted they fulfill one of the diagnostic criteria for anorexia, an increasingly common psychiatric disease most commonly affecting young women. It is associated with multisystem dysfunction and associated with an increased morbidity and mortality from suicide or from organ failure due to starvation. Anorexics tend to have a resting bradycardia, hypotension and impaired ventricular function. The patient's eating pattern may be very erratic and a good history may be difficult to obtain; however, as gastric emptying is delayed and gut motility diminished, it is wise to assume that the stomach may not have emptied normally following food.

Adults tend to increase their weight gradually with age, and the genetic contribution to body weight is estimated to be the most important factor, environmental factors producing approximately 30% of the effect.

The body mass index is the body weight in kilograms divided by the height squared in metres. The normal is approximately 24, obesity is at levels > 28 and morbid obesity is > 35.

Q3.7

A = False
B = False
C = True
D = True
E = True

Mountain sickness occurs 8–24 hours after arriving at high altitude (i.e. at altitude > 3700m) and lasts 4–8 days. It presents as headache, insomnia, irritability, dyspnoea, nausea and vomiting. Cerebral oedema may occur. Treatment includes rest, oxygen, acetazolamide and steroids. Acetazolamide is a carbonic anhydrase inhibitor which can be given orally or IV, acetaminophen is paracetamol. Physiological changes include increased alveolar ventilation in response to the decreased PaO_2 (hypoxic drive) and therefore a respiratory alkalosis. This results in a decreased central drive for respiration, and the cerebrospinal fluid HCO_3^- shows a compensatory decrease. There is stimulation of the bone marrow to increase erythropoeitin and so red cell production, resulting in long term polycythaemia. There is an increase in pulmonary blood flow and pulmonary oedema may occur. Artificial ventilation and transfer to a lower altitude may be necessary in severe cases. Pulmonary oedema is treated with rest, O_2 and nifedipine.

Q3.8

A = False
B = False
C = False
D = True
E = True

The residual volume is the volume of the lungs after a maximal expiratory effort, and is approximately 1.2 litre in the adult. The functional residual capacity is the volume in the lungs at the end of quiet expiration, i.e. the sum of the residual volume and the expiratory reserve volume.

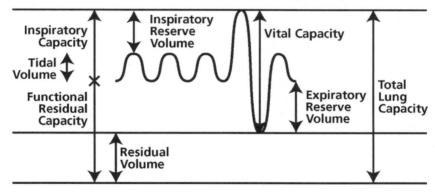

Fig. 3.1: Lung volumes and capacities

(N.B. a capacity is the sum of two or more volumes). The vital capacity is the sum of the inspiratory reserve volume and the expiratory reserve volume and the tidal volume.

Q3.9

A = True
B = False
C = True
D = True
E = False

Pain from pinprick, heat and strong pressure is transmitted from the mechanoreceptors in the skin via Aδ fibres to the lamina I of the dorsal horn. Duller aching pain is transmitted from the polymodal nocioceptors in most tissues, via slower unmyelinated C fibres to the lamina II in the dorsal horn and the substantia gelatinosa, where both fibres synapse and cross the spinal cord to ascend in the spinothalamic tracts to the thalamus and the sensory cortex. Within the dorsal horn the main neurotransmitter is substance P; however, many other transmitters function there too, including angiotensin II, cholecystokinin, 5HT, and noradrenaline. Most descending pathways are inhibitory in nature, affecting pain by 'closing the gate' and diminishing transmission of the stimulus.

Q3.10
A = True
B = False
C = True
D = False
E = True

The nicotinic acetylcholine receptor is a protein with a molecular weight of 250 000. It contains five subunits, two alpha, 1 beta, one gamma in the foetus (epsilon in the adult) and one delta. These subunits extend through the cell membrane around the sodium channel. Each alpha subunit may bind one acetylcholine molecule, and when both binding sites are filled the resulting configurational change results in opening of the central sodium channel. Acetylcholine, the transmitter at these junctions, it is released in response to a nerve impulse causing calcium to enter the nerve terminal, which in turn causes marked increase in release of the acetylcholine present in vesicles. Its activity is terminated by metabolism by cholinesterases to choline and acetate within the neuromuscular junction. Pseudocholinesterase is found in plasma and is a relatively nonspecific cholinesterase.

Q3.11
A = False
B = True
C = False
D = False
E = False

The carotid bodies are situated near the carotid bifurcation on each side of the neck. Aortic bodies occur near the arch of the aorta. Both the carotid and aortic bodies are involved in the control of ventilation and respond to decreases in arterial oxygenation and pH. In the carotid bodies this results in increased firing. The impulses are transmitted via the glossopharyngeal nerves to the respiratory centre of the medulla, resulting in increased ventilation. The blood flow to the carotid bodies is 2000 ml $100g^{-1}$ min^{-1} (a carotid body weighs approximately 2 mg). That of the brain is 50 ml $100g^{-1}$ min^{-1}, and of the heart 65 ml $100g^{-1}$ min^{-1}. The carotid sinus, not the carotid body, responds to changes in blood pressure.

Q3.12
A = False
B = True
C = False
D = True
E = False

Characteristically there are three waves and two descents in the jugular venous pulse: the 'a' wave is the result of atrial systole, and the 'c' wave is due to the closing of the tricuspid valve back into the atrium (causing a rise in atrial pressure) during ventricular contraction and prior to opening of the pulmonary valve. The following 'x' descent is due to atrial relaxation. The 'v' wave is due to increased atrial filling from the great veins prior to opening of the tricuspid valve, and this in turn is followed by the 'y' descent, which corresponds to opening of the tricuspid valve and passage of blood from the right atrium to the ventricle. Giant 'a' waves occur when the atria contract against a closed tricuspid valve in complete heart block or during junctional rhythm in which the atrium and ventricle are activated simultaneously.

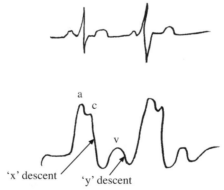

Fig. 3.2: Jugular venous pulse

Q3.13
A = True
B = True
C = True
D = False
E = True

During starvation, when there is insufficient calorie intake, proteins are catabolised for energy. There is a protein-sparing effect in the presence of small amounts of glucose as the resultant increased insulin production inhibits the catabolism of protein. The catabolised protein mainly comes from muscle, liver and spleen, with sparing of protein in the heart and brain.

Ketone levels rise as fat is metabolised, and they can be used as energy substrates in the brain. If there is no food intake then death from starvation will occur in approximately 60 days, provided there is fluid intake.

During starvation the basal metabolic rate decreases in response to a fall in T3. This helps conserve proteins and calories, because of a decrease in the conversion of T4 (thyroxine) to T3 (triiodothyrodine), the latter being normally the more active hormone.

Q3.14
A = False
B = True
C = False
D = False
E = False

Parathyroid hormone (PTH) secretion is governed by ionised calcium levels. PTH release is increased by hypocalcaemia and hypomagnesaemia, allowing mobilisation of calcium from the bone. Clinical signs of hypocalcaemia include tetany, Chvostek's sign of facial contraction produced by gentle tapping the facial nerve at the angle of the jaw, and Trousseau's sign which is spasm of the hand due to tetany.

Hyperparathyroidism due to renal disease and a loss of sensitivity to 1,25 dihydroxycholecalciferol results in chronic hypocalcaemia causing parathyroid hypertrophy. Pseudohyperparathyroidism is associated with normal or increased levels of PTH but failure of response of the tissues to the hormone due to lack of receptor sensitivity.

Calcitonin is produced in the parafollicular cells of the thyroid. Calcitonin secretion causes a lowering of the plasma calcium and phosphate, increases urinary excretion of calcium, and inhibits bone resorbtion.

Q3.15
A = True
B = True
C = True
D = True
E = True

The sympathetic and parasympathetic systems make up the autonomic nervous system. Transmitters at the sympathetic nerve endings include acetylcholine, noradrenaline and dopamine. α2 receptors are stimulated by clonidine and α1 receptors are stimulated by methoxamine and phenylephrine. Both bretylium and guanethidine block noradrenaline release.

The parasympathetic tracts are made up of a cranial outflow from the midbrain and medulla and the sacral outflow from S234.

Q3.16
A = True
B = True
C = False
D = True
E = False

Intramuscular blood flow decreases as the vessels become compressed by increasing muscle tension. The increased blood flow to muscle with exercise occurs predominately between contractions. This change is mediated by both sympathetic stimulation and local metabolic conditions. The cardiac output increases greatly during exercise through an increase in both heart rate and stroke volume. Trained athletes have a slower heart rate and larger stroke volume both at rest and during exercise, and also have more efficient oxygen extraction at tissue level.

Local factors leading to an increase in blood flow and availability of oxygen to exercising muscle include low tissue PO_2, increased tissue PCO_2, decreased pH, increased plasma potassium, elevated temperature; there is also an increase in 2,3-DPG and a shift to the right of the oxygen dissociation curve.

Q3.17
A = True
B = True
C = False
D = False
E = True

ADH is a polypeptide secreted by the posterior pituitary gland. It acts to increase the permeability of the collecting ducts of the kidney, resulting in water retention and the excretion of a concentrated urine. Increased plasma oncotic pressure, pain, stress, exercise, nausea and vomiting, standing, morphine, barbiturates and angiotensin II stimulate secretion of ADH. Secretion is decreased by decreased osmotic pressure, increased extracellular fluid volume and alcohol.

Q3.18
A = False
B = True
C = False
D = False
E = False

The oxygen dissociation curve is shifted to the right by a decrease in pH, an increase in temperature, increased 2,3-DPG level (which is produced by ascent to high altitude), thyroxine, growth hormone, androgens and exercise. This shift to the right means that the haemoglobin affinity for oxygen is decreased and more oxygen is liberated for the tissues.

A shift to the left, which increases the affinity of haemoglobin for oxygen, is produced by alkalosis, hypothermia and decreased levels of 2,3-DPG (e.g. in stored blood). Hyperkalaemia does not in itself affect the position of the curve, but if it is associated with acidosis the curve will be shifted to the right.

# Q3.19
A = True
B = False
C = False
D = True
E = True

In the normal erect lung, due to the effects of gravity, both ventilation and perfusion are greatest at the bases. On travelling towards the apices, both ventilation and perfusion decrease. The decrease in ventilation is less than the decrease in perfusion, which results in an increasing ventilation–perfusion mismatch. If perfusion is decreased relative to ventilation the alveolar pCO_2 decreases because less carbon dioxide is delivered to the alveoli, while the alveolar pO_2 rises as less enters the bloodstream. Thus the alveolar pCO_2 is the least and the alveolar pO_2 the greatest at the apex.

At the apices the pulmonary artery pressure is normally just sufficient to maintain adequate perfusion. If hypotension occurs, although the apical alveoli will still be ventilated they will not be perfused and an increase in the physiological deadspace will occur.

The lung can be divided into three zones:

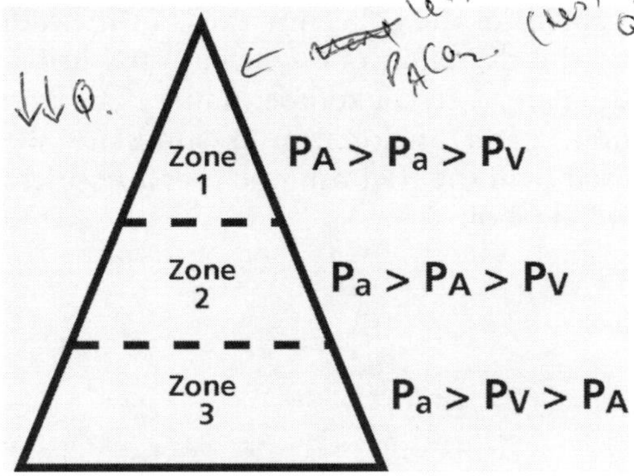

Fig. 3.3: Zones of the lung

i   Zone one at the apex where the alveolar pressure (P_A) > the arterial pressure (P_a) > the venous pressure (P_V) and therefore there is no blood flow; this contributes to the physiological dead space. (This zone does not exist under normal conditions.)

ii   Zone two at the mid-portion of the lung where $P_a > P_A > P_V$, thus blood flow is dependent upon the difference between arterial and alveolar pressures.

iii   Zone three at the bases where $P_a > P_V > P_A$, thus blood flow is determined in the usual manner by the arteriovenous pressure difference.

Q3.20
A = True
B = True
C = True
D = True
E = True

Physical effects of hypoxia include headache, drowsiness, disorientation, anorexia, nausea, vomiting, tachycardia, tachypnoea and hypertension. It essentially causes vasodilatation in all parts of the circulation except the pulmonary vessels, which respond to hypoxia by vasoconstriction (hypoxic pulmonary vasoconstriction). The vasoconstriction which occurs in the pulmonary circulation is a protective mechanism designed to divert blood away from locally hypoxic and therefore unventilated areas of lung.

The vasoconstriction in the peripheries is counteracted by reflex cerebral vasodilatation mediated via the sympathetic nervous system in order to maintain cerebral blood flow.

Q3.21
A = True
B = False
C = True
D = True
E = True

Cardiac muscle, like skeletal muscle, compresses its blood vessels when it contracts, thus coronary blood flow occurs predominately in diastole and is approximately $250\,\mathrm{ml\,min^{-1}}$. As diastole is shorter during a tachycardia, coronary blood flow is reduced. It is also decreased by reductions in diastolic pressure and increases in venous pressure (e.g. in cardiac failure), as both of these effectively reduce the coronary perfusion pressure. Local mediators also play a role in coronary perfusion; vasodilatation is produced by local hypoxia, hypercapnia, acidosis, hyperkalaemia, prostaglandins and adenosine.

Q3.22
A = False
B = True
C = True
D = True
E = True

The transmitter at all autonomic ganglia, including the adrenal medulla, is acetylcholine. It occurs at the nerve terminals in synaptic vesicles. Postganglionic parasympathetic nerves are also cholinergic, as are motor nerves supplying skeletal muscle and postganglionic sympathetic nerves supplying sweat glands. The remaining postganglionic sympathetic nerves release noradrenaline and adrenaline as their neurotransmitters.

Many other neurotransmitters have been identified, including dopamine, noradrenaline, 5HT, adenosine, glutamate and GABA, each acting at various specific receptors. Acetylcholine receptors are divided into muscarinic and nicotinic types. The muscarinic receptors are further divided into at least five subtypes, M_1 to M_5.

Q3.23
A = True
B = False
C = False
D = True
E = True

Thyroxine (T4) is a modified amino acid, synthesised by iodination of the amino acid tyrosine. Circulating thyroxine is 99.98% protein-bound to thyroid-binding globulin (thyroglobulin), albumin and prealbumin (transthyretin). T3 is also highly protein-bound. T3 is 3–5 times as potent as T4, acts more rapidly and is thought to be the active metabolite. Plasma TSH levels regulate thyroid function; increased TSH causes increased secretion of thyroxine, which in turn feeds back to decrease the release of TSH by the anterior pituitary gland.

Q3.24
A = False
B = True
C = False
D = True
E = True

Erythropoietin is a glycoprotein whose production is stimulated by anaemia or local tissue hypoxia. It acts to increase erythropoiesis in the bone marrow. Synthetic formulations (epoetin = recombinant human erythropoietin) are now available and it is used in the treatment of chronic anaemia, such as that of renal disease, and in patients who aim to avoid blood transfusion despite blood loss, such as Jehovah's Witness patients undergoing extensive surgery or patients undergoing some chemotherapeutic regimes.

Erythropoietin increases the rate of production of red blood cells in response to hypoxia or hypovolaemia. In adults, 85% of erythropoietin is produced by the kidney and 15% by the liver, thus when its production is reduced by renal failure anaemia will result. Production of erythropoietin is also stimulated by androgens, alkalosis, catecholamines and adenosine but inhibited by theophylline. In the foetus the normally low PaO_2 leads to an increased level of erythropoietin and therefore high haemoglobin levels at birth. The subsequent increase in PaO_2 on delivery causes a decrease in erythropoietin and the haemoglobin naturally decreases to its lowest level at about 8 weeks of age, when erythropoietin production once again increases.

Q3.25
A = False
B = True
C = True
D = False
E = True

The alpha cells of the islets of Langerhans in the pancreas and the upper gastrointestinal tract produce glucagon, a polypeptide. Glucagon acts to oppose insulin and increase blood glucose by increasing gluconeogenesis in the liver. It promotes glycogenolysis. It also increases lipolysis and increases the metabolic rate. It acts as a neurotransmitter in the retina and hypothalamus, and in large doses is an inotrope, increasing contractility without increasing myocardial excitability.

Glucagon can be used in the management of hypoglycaemia, as it increases the blood glucose level by mobilising glycogen stores in the liver.

Q3.26
A = True
B = True
C = False
D = True
E = False

There are three types of muscle: skeletal, cardiac and smooth. Cardiac and skeletal are striated, whereas smooth is not. The individual cardiac fibres are linked together by intercalated discs, which help to maintain intracellular cohesion. Fibre contraction is initiated by depolarisation of the motor end plate producing action potentials in the muscle fibres. This leads to release of calcium from the sarcoplasmic reticulum, which enables the active formation of cross linkages between actin and myosin filaments and subsequent shortening of the fibre. The process is terminated by the active re-uptake of calcium by the sarcoplasmic reticulum.

Q3.27
A = True
B = False
C = False
D = False
E = False

The normal range for serum potassium is 3.8–5.0 mmol litre^{-1}, and for sodium 138–142 mmol litre^{-1}. Correct diagnosis and management of such abnormalities in plasma electrolytes is important.

Addison's disease is the result of destruction of the whole adrenal cortex so that glucocorticoid, mineralocorticoid and sex hormone production are all reduced. The decrease in mineralocorticoid element classically results in low sodium and high potassium. Excess aldosterone secretion, as in Conn's syndrome, results in potassium depletion and sodium retention; similarly but to a lesser extent the mineralocorticoid effects of cortisol in Cushing's disease may cause sodium retention and potassium loss. In hypopituitarism, although ACTH secretion is reduced, mineralocorticoid function by the adrenal cortex is normal and therefore electrolyte imbalance is uncommon. Acute renal failure may present with hyperkalaemia but is unlikely to produce a serum sodium as low as 120 mmol litre^{-1}.

Q3.28
A = False
B = True
C = True
D = False
E = True

The taste buds are situated on the fungiform and circumvallate papillae, not the filiform papillae. The reticular activating system takes input from the many different sensory pathways and is integral in allowing perception of consciousness. GABA is an inhibitory mediator which acts as a neurotransmitter at GABA$_A$, and GABA$_B$ receptors present mainly in the brain and retina. Benzodiazepines act at benzodiazapine receptors located at GABA receptors. Angiotensin II is one of the most powerful vasoconstrictors known, being 4–8 times more potent than adrenaline. Over 500 ml of CSF is produced by the choroid plexus in the adult per day. It is constantly resorbed into the venous system via the arachnoid villi and therefore the ventricles and subarachnoid spaces usually contain approximately 150 ml. If resorption is restricted there is accumulation of CSF, which results in hydrocephalus and raised intracranial pressure.

Q3.29
A = False
B = False
C = False
D = True
E = True

The adrenal gland is divided into the inner medulla and outer cortex. The medulla functions as a sympathetic ganglion in which the postganglionic cells have no axons and upon stimulation secrete adrenaline, noradrenaline and dopamine. The outer adrenal cortex is essential for life, secreting glucocorticoids, a mineralocorticoid and sex hormones. The cortex is divided into three zones: the outer zona glomerulosa, the middle zona fascicularis and the inner zona reticularis. All three zones secrete corticosterone and the fascicularis and reticularis secrete cortisol and sex hormones.

Q3.30
A = True
B = False
C = True
D = False
E = False

Foetal haemoglobin (HbF) makes up 50% of the haemoglobin concentration at birth. HbF decreases to about 5% by 5 months and to less than 2% by 2 years.

HbF is raised in 50% of patients with thalassaemia minor, and in all with thalassaemia major. It is also raised in many conditions including sickle cell disease, pernicious anaemia, multiple myeloma and some leukaemias.

Polycythaemia is defined as a haemoglobin level of $18–24 \, g \, dl^{-1}$. It may be primary or secondary. Secondary polycythaemia results from chronic hypoxia (as found when living at altitude), in patients with cyanotic cardiac disease, chronic respiratory disease (e.g. emphysema, chronic pulmonary emboli or primary pulmonary hypertension).

In sickle cell trait, electrophoresis reveals 20%–40% HbS, and 60%–80% HbA and < 2% HbF, in sickle cell anaemia HbS levels are 80%–100%; the difference is made up by HbF.

Following an acute bleed the blood film will show a normochromic, normocytic picture. There is an increase in the reticulocyte count within a couple of days but it may take up to 8 weeks for the haemoglobin levels to return to normal.

4. Applied Pharmacology

Q4.1 **The following agents are administered as single isomer preparations:**

A. cisatracurium
B. mivacurium
C. ropivicaine
D. atracurium
E. remifentanil

Q4.2 **A patient with a dibucaine number of 15–25 and fluoride number of 20 will have delayed recovery from the following agents:**

A. cisatracurium
B. mivacurium
C. remifentanil
D. suxamethonium
E. rocuronium

Q4.3 **Concerning inhalational agents:**

A. xenon has minimum alveolar concentration (MAC) 71 and blood/gas solubility coefficient 0.14
B. sevofluorane has MAC 6 and blood/gas solubility 0.42
C. desflurane has MAC 2.5 and blood/gas solubility 0.69
D. compound A accumulation is a potential risk when sevoflurane is used with low flow anaesthesia
E. desflurane does not trigger malignant hyperpyrexia in susceptible patients

Q4.4 Regarding propofol:

A. the Bristol regimen for maintenance of anaesthesia is $14\,mg\,kg^{-1}$ for 15 minutes, then $10\,mg\,kg^{-1}$ for 10 minutes, then $6\,mg\,kg^{-1}$ thereafter
B. blood concentrations of $10\,\mu g\,ml^{-1}$ are generally required for induction of anaesthesia
C. target controlled infusion (TCI) devices require the patient's age, weight, and gender to adjust infusion rates
D. propofol is licensed for sedation in children over the age of 3 years
E. propofol is contraindicated in epilepsy

Q4.5 The following drugs are licensed for intrathecal administration:

A. remifentanil
B. hyperbaric bupivicaine
C. morphine
D. fentanyl
E. clonidine

Q4.6 Ketamine hydrochloride:

A. is a phencyclidine derivative
B. is an agonist at NMDA receptors
C. is antanalgesic
D. the $S(+)$ isomer is more potent than the $R(-)$ isomer
E. decreases cerebral blood flow

Q4.7 Neuroleptic malignant syndrome (NMS):

A. is treated with dantrolene
B. may be triggered by metoclopramide
C. has a rapid onset, usually within one hour of trigger
D. is mediated via N-Methyl-D-Aspartate (NMDA) receptors
E. is associated with thromboembolism

Q4.8 Coagulation is affected in the following ways:

A. tranexamic acid increases fibrinolysis
B. aprotonin activates kallikrein
C. low molecular weight heparin inhibits platelet aggregation more than unfractionated heparin
D. protamine has anticoagulant activity at high doses
E. vasopressin causes increased levels of factor VIII

Q4.9 In the management of acute pain:

A. rofecoxib is contraindicated in patients with active peptic ulceration
B. tramadol enhances 5-hydroxytryptamine (5-HT) release
C. coproxamol contains 500 mg paracetamol
D. subarachnoid clonidine may cause hypotension
E. nabilone is licensed for the treatment of chronic pain

Q4.10 The following statements concerning drugs acting on the cardiovascular system are true:

A. lisinopril causes hypokalaemia
B. enoximone causes vasodilation
C. amiodarone has a half-life of 10 hours
D. losartan is a calcium channel antagonist
E. dopexamine is an agonist at β_2-adrenergic receptors

Q4.11 Treatment with frusemide can cause the following:

A. hypercalcaemia
B. hypomagnasaemia
C. hyperuricaemia
D. hypoglycaemia
E. hyponatraemia

Q4.12 Hypokalaemia is a recognised complication of:

A. treatment with digoxin
B. treatment with amiloride
C. villous papillomata of the rectum
D. severe acidosis
E. treatment with bleomycin

Q4.13 In acute porphyria the following drugs may be safely prescribed:

A. pethidine
B. diazepam
C. thiopentone
D. methyldopa
E. phenytoin

Q4.14 The following are considered the maximum safe doses for a 70 kg man:

A. lignocaine 4 ml of 4%
B. ropivicaine 5 mg kg^{-1}
C. prilocaine with adrenaline 60 ml of 1%
D. bupivicaine 40 ml of 0.5%
E. cocaine 10 ml of 10%

Q4.15 In a patient taking monoamine oxidase inhibitors, the following are contraindicated:

A. pethidine
B. allopurinol
C. ephedrine
D. pickled herrings
E. ketamine

Q4.16 Digoxin:

A. delays atrioventricular conduction
B. toxicity is common when the plasma magnesium level is
   > 1.0 mmol litre^{-1}
C. is a positive inotrope
D. is the treatment of choice in Wolff–Parkinson–White syndrome
E. is the treatment of choice in severe bradycardia

Q4.17 Metopralol tartrate:

A. is a nonselective beta-blocker
B. decreases airway resistance
C. can be used in the management of migraine
D. is contraindicated in second degree heart block
E. causes hyperglycaemia

Q4.18 The following statements are true:

A. esmolol is a selective β_2 adrenergic agonist
B. bromocriptine is a dopamine antagonist
C. metformin is a sulphonylurea
D. phenoxybenzamine is an α-adrenergic antagonist
E. clomiphine is an α-adrenergic agonist

Q4.19 Which of the following statements are correct:

A. zero-order kinetics means that a constant amount of drug is eliminated per unit time
B. first-order kinetics means that a constant fraction of the total dose of the drug is eliminated per unit time
C. a volume of distribution greater than the total body fluid volume implies drug concentration in the tissues
D. the plasma half-life of a drug is the time required for half of the administered drug dose to be eliminated from the body
E. clearance is the rate of elimination of the drug multiplied by the concentration of the drug in the plasma

Q4.20 Calcium channel blockers:

A. are class IV antidysrhythmic agents
B. decrease lower oesophageal sphincter tone
C. may reduce mortality following subarachnoid haemorrhage
D. can precipitate symptoms of toxicity in patients taking digoxin
E. may be indicated in the management of Raynaud's disease

Q4.21 The following are features of severe salicylate poisoning in adults:

A. confusion
B. fever
C. respiratory acidosis
D. dry skin
E. vomiting

Q4.22 A patient on phenelzine is given an injection of ephedrine. He develops a blood pressure of 270/160. Treatment may include:

A. labetolol
B. methoxamine
C. phentolamine
D. diazoxide
E. guanethidine

Q4.23 The early signs (within 24 hours) of paracetamol overdose include:

A. increased AST levels
B. nausea and vomiting
C. bleeding tendency
D. metabolic acidosis
E. hepatic encephalopathy

Q4.24 Parenteral nutrition:

A. must be delivered into a central vein
B. should provide at least 0.2 g of nitrogen per kg per day for basal requirements
C. may be monitored with weekly serum electrolyte measurement
D. is without complications in modern practice
E. should not be given to patients with renal failure

Q4.25 The following drugs are metabolised by plasma cholinesterase:

A. esmolol
B. suxamethonium
C. amethocaine
D. ecothiopate eye drops
E. etomidate

Q4.26 In renal failure there is impaired excretion of:

A. digoxin
B. warfarin
C. tubocurare
D. morphine
E. gentamicin

Q4.27 The following exhibit significant first-pass metabolism:

A. aspirin
B. morphine
C. lignocaine
D. glyceryl trinitrate
E. frusemide

Q4.28 Carbamazepine may be useful in the management of:

A. trigeminal neuralgia
B. manic depression
C. glossopharyngeal neuralgia
D. thalamic pain
E. phantom limb pain

Q4.29 Heparin:

A. one unit of heparin is the amount required to prevent 1.0 ml of sheep blood from clotting for one hour following the addition of 0.2 ml of 1/100 calcium chloride solution
B. forms a complex with antithrombin III which inhibits factors Xa and thrombin
C. has a molecular weight of 2000–5000
D. may cause thrombocytopaenia
E. may be reversed by intravenous vitamin K

Q4.30 The following drugs should be discontinued before anaesthesia for elective laparascopic cholecystectomy:

A. clonidine
B. tranylcypromine
C. imipramine
D. progesterone-only oral contraceptive pill
E. prednisolone

Answers to Section 4

Q4.1
A = True
B = False
C = True
D = False
E = False
Isomers are drugs with the same molecular weight and chemical composition, but which differ in the precise arrangement of their individual atoms or groups. In general, three types of isomerism occur with drugs; structural, dynamic and stereo. Stereo-isomerism can be further divided into optical and geometric.

Optical isomerism refers to the phenomenon of chirality (handedness) where a drug can exist in right- or left-handed forms which may have different effects on enzymes and receptors. S(+) ketamine produces more amnesia and anaesthesia than the R(−) isomer, with fewer emergence phenomena and faster recovery. *l*-bupivicaine has fewer side effects than the traditional racemic preparation of *l*- and *R*-bupivicaine. *Cis-trans*-isomerism refers to the arrangements of paired atoms or groups around a double bond; *cis*- refers to both substituents being on the same side, while *trans*- refers to one being on each side.

Q4.2
A = False
B = True
C = False
D = True
E = False
Genetic polymorphism exists for the expression of plasma cholinesterase, and the most common genetic variant (the atypical enzyme) can be distinguished from the usual enzyme by its resistance to inhibition by the local anaesthetic cinchocaine (dibucaine). The dibucaine number is the percentage inhibition of plasma cholinesterase produced by a standard titre of dibucaine (10^{-5}M) using benzoyl-choline as a substrate. The fluoride number is the percentage inhibition of plasma cholinesterase by fluoride (10^{-5}M). A normal dibucaine number (normal homozygotes) is approximately 80%, and a normal fluoride number is about 60%. For the DD genotype (homozygotes for the atypical enzyme) the dibucaine number will be about 20% (and so will the fluoride number); for the FF genotype (heterozygotes

for the atypical enzyme) the dibucaine number is about 60% and the fluoride number is about 20%.

Remifentanil is metabolised by erythrocyte cholinesterase, not plasma enzyme. Mivacurium and suxamethonium are metabolised by plasma cholinesterase and therefore would have prolonged action in the example given. Rocuronium is primarily excreted by the liver, and cis-atracurium is mostly metabolised by Hofmann degredation.

Q4.3
A = True
B = False
C = False
D = True
E = False

Desflurane has MAC 6 and blood/gas solubility 0.42, sevoflurane has MAC 2.5 and blood/gas solubility 0.69.

Compound A (pentafluoroisopropenyl fluoromethyl ether) is more likely to be produced at high temperatures, high concentrations of sevoflurane, with the use of baralyme and at very low flows. It has been shown to be toxic in rats, causing renal, hepatic and cerebral damage. However, it has not proven harmful in clinical practice with humans even with high-dose sevoflurane at low flow.

All inhalational anaesthetic agents may act as trigger agents for malignant hyperpyrexia.

Q4.4
A = False
B = False
C = False
D = False
E = False

The maintenance of anaesthesia with propofol may be achieved by various regimens based on pharmacokinetic studies. The Bristol regimen is commonly used; $10\,mg\,kg^{-1}\,h^{-1}$ for 10 minutes, then $8\,mg\,kg^{-1}\,h^{-1}$ for 10 minutes, followed by $6\,mg\,kg^{-1}\,h^{-1}$ thereafter, adjusted if required according to clinical response. This regimen includes the use of 66% N_2O in oxygen or an infusion of alfentanil $30–50\,\mu g\,kg^{-1}\,h^{-1}$.

Target controlled infusion devices are available in which prefilled syringes of propofol are loaded and infusion rates automatically adjusted according to the patient's age, weight and required blood concentrations of propofol. A propofol blood concentration of $4–8\,\mu g\,ml^{-1}$ is required for induction and

3–6 µg ml^{-1} for maintenance of anaesthesia in healthy adults.

Propofol is not licensed for use in children under 3 years of age, or for sedation of children of any age, as neurological, cardiac, renal and hepatic impairment have been reported after sedation of children with propofol in ICUs. Propofol has been used successfully to treat status epilepticus. Convulsions have been reported following its use but a causative role has not been proven.

Q4.5
A = False
B = True
C = False
D = False
E = False
Remifentanil formulation contains glycine and is therefore not recommended for spinal or epidural administration. Although commonly used as adjuncts in spinal anaesthesia and analgesia, opioids, ketamine, midazolam and clonidine are not licensed for use by this route.

Q4.6
A = True
B = False
C = False
D = True
E = False
Ketamine hydrochloride is a phencylidine ('angel dust') derivative but is less hallucinogenic. It is an antagonist at N-Methyl-D-Aspartate (NMDA) receptors to cause analgesia and dissociative anaesthesia. The commercial preparation is a racemic mixture of two isomers with similar pharmacokinetic properties but the S(+) isomer is 2–4 times as potent as the R(−) isomer, and less psychoactive with more rapid recovery.

Blood pressure and heart rate are usually increased, as is cerebral blood flow.

Q4.7
A = True
B = True
C = False
D = False
E = True
Neuroleptic malignant syndrome (NMS) is rare and is characterised by altered consciousness, hyperthermia, autonomic dysfunction and muscle

rigidity. Trigger agents include butyrophenones, phenothiazines, withdrawal of L-dopa in patients with Parkinson's disease, metoclopramide, lithium and reserpine. It is thought to be related to the antidoperminergic activity of the drugs. Features develop over 1–3 days and treatment is supportive, with supplemental oxygen, cooling, hydration and venous thromboembolism prophylaxis. Agents which increase central dopaminergic activity have been used (e.g. bromocriptine, amantadine and L-dopa). Dantrolene may be used to treat the peripheral muscle effects. Mortality is 20%–30% from renal failure, arrhythmias, pulmonary embolus or aspiration pneumonitis.

Q4.8
A = False
B = False
C = False
D = True
E = True

Tranexamic acid is an antifibrinolytic drug. Aprotonin may be used to reduce perioperative blood loss; it is a serine protease inhibitor which inhibits plasmin at low doses thus reducing fibrinolysis. At higher doses, aprotonin inhibits kallikrein, causing anticoagulation; it also inhibits trypsin. Intermediate doses cause reduced platelet aggregation.

Heparin accelerates the action of antithrombin III, thus inhibiting the action of factors XII, XI, IX, X and thrombin; it also inhibits platelet aggregation by fibrin. Low-molecular-weight heparin is fractionated and has a more specific effect on factor X. This results in fewer systemic anticoagulant effects, less effect on platelet function, a longer $t_{\frac{1}{2}}$ and fewer haemorrhagic effects than unfractionated heparin. Protamine, a mixture of low-molecular-weight cationic basic proteins prepared from the sperm of salmon and other fish, binds and inactivates anionic acidic heparin to form a stable salt. In high doses it has an anticoagulant effect by inhibiting the formation and action of thromboplastin. Vasopressin causes water retention, vasoconstriction and an increase in the plasma levels of factor VIII. It is used therapeutically as desmopressin in the treatment of haemophilia and von Willebrand's disease.

Q4.9
A = True
B = True
C = False
D = True
E = False

Rofecoxib is a cyclo-oxygenase-2 (COX-2) selective inhibitor with similar analgesic effect to the non-selective diclofenac. The selectivity for COX-2 should confer advantages with respect to the gastric toxicity of non-selective COX inhibitors; this has yet to be proven. National Institute for Clinical Excellence (NICE) guidance is to use COX-2 inhibitors in preference to standard NSAIDs only when clearly indicated for patients with a history of peptic ulceration, perforation or bleeding. It is contraindicated in patients with active peptic ulceration or gastrointestinal bleeding.

Tramadol hydrochloride is an opioid analgesic which also inhibits noradrenaline uptake and enhances 5-HT release. It has fewer of the typical opioid side effects (notably, respiratory depression, constipation and addiction potential), but is not as effective in severe postoperative pain as morphine.

Compound analgesic agents contain a simple analgesic such as paracetamol with an opioid component. Coproxamol contains dextropropoxyphene hydrochloride 32.5 mg and paracetamol 325 mg. The advantages of compound prescribing have not been substantiated as the ability to titrate the individual doses to pain is reduced. Also, the management of overdose may be complicated.

Clonidine hydrochloride is an α-adrenergic receptor agonist. It may be used as an anti-hypertensive agent and as an adjunct to analgesia. It acts centrally by stimulating presynaptic α_2-adrenergic receptors. The mechanism of action for its analgesic and sedative properties is not clear.

Nabilone is a synthetic cannabinoid with antiemetic properties and may be used for nausea and vomiting caused by cytotoxic chemotherapy that is unresponsive to conventional antiemetics. The main psychoactive chemical in cannabis is δ-9-terahydrocannabinol. Possible therapeutic uses include antiemesis, analgesia, anticonvulsant and anti-muscle spasm. Present law prohibits the prescription of cannabis without a Home Office licence, and meaningful trials supportive of its use are yet to be completed.

Q4.10
A = False
B = True
C = False
D = False
E = True

Lisinopril is an angiotensin-converting enzyme (ACE) inhibitor. ACE converts angiotensin I to angiotensin II, and breaks down kinins, naturally occuring vasodilators. Hypokalaemia does not result from its administration.

Enoximone is a phosphodiesterase inhibitor with direct action on cardiac muscle leading to increase contractility. It may also cause peripheral vasodilatation and is often referred to as an 'inodilator'.

Amiodarone is a class III anti-arrhythmic agent with a half-life of 10–100 days.

Losartan is a specific angiotensin-II-receptor antagonist with many properties similar to the ACE inhibitors. It does not, however, inhibit the breakdown of bradykinin and other kinins and therefore does not cause the persistent dry cough often seen with ACE inhibitor therapy.

Dopexamine is an analogue of dopamine and stimulates β_2-adrenergic receptors in addition to peripheral dopamine receptors.

Q4.11
A = False
B = True
C = True
D = False
E = True

Loop diuretics (e.g. frusemide, bumetanide and ethacrynic acid) inhibit active chloride reabsorption in the thick portion of the ascending limb of the loop of Henle. This results in increased urinary excretion of sodium, calcium, potassium and magnesium. By reducing the tonicity of the renal medulla, a hypotonic or isotonic urine is produced. Hyperuricaemia also occurs and may precipitate an acute attack in patients with pre-existing gout. Frusemide causes metabolic alkalosis and may be diabetogenic, but hypoglycaemia is not a complication of frusemide therapy. Transient auditory nerve damage, pancreatitis and bone marrow depression have all been reported with frusemide therapy.

Q4.12
A = False
B = False
C = True
D = False
E = True

Hypokalaemia may be due to excessive loss from the body, inadequate intake, or intracellular redistribution, of potassium. Amiloride is a potassium-sparing diuretic which tends to avoid the hypokalaemia associated with thiazide and loop diuretics. Villous papillomata will cause increased losses of potassium from the gut. Severe acidosis results in translocation of potassium from the intracellular to the extracellular space, causing hyperkalaemia. Digoxin does not cause potassium loss, but digoxin toxicity is more likely in the presence of hypokalaemia.

Q4.13
A = True
B = True
C = False
D = True
E = False
Porphyria is a group of inborn errors of porphyrin metabolism (pigmented compounds produced in haemoprotein synthesis). It is caused by specific enzyme defects within the haem metabolic pathway. There are several forms of the disease, divided into hepatic and erythropoietic varieties. There are three forms affecting the conduct of anaesthesia, all hepatic and inherited as autosomal-dominant conditions: acute intermittent porphyria, variegate porphyria and hereditary coproporphyria. Presentation may be with abdominal pain, nausea and vomiting, confusion, psychosis, seizures, motor neuropathy and hypotension. Acute attacks may be precipitated by drugs, stress, infection, alcohol ingestion, menstruation, pregnancy and starvation, although not at every exposure. Drug precipitants include barbiturates, phenytoin, sulphonamides, pancuronium, griseofulvin, oestrogens and alcohol.

Q4.14
A = True
B = False
C = True
D = False
E = False
The maximum documented safe doses of commonly used local anaesthetic agents include:
- Lignocaine 3 mg kg^{-1}, lignocaine with adrenaline 7 mg kg^{-1}
- Prilocaine 5 mg kg^{-1}, prilocaine with adrenaline 8 mg kg^{-1}
- Bupivicaine 2 mg kg^{-1}
- Cocaine 1.5 mg kg^{-1}
- Ropivicaine 3.5 mg kg^{-1}

N.B. A 1% solution contains 10 mg ml^{-1}.

Q4.15
A = True
B = False
C = True
D = True
E = True
Monoamine oxidase inhibitors (MAOIs) interact with a variety of drugs and foodstuffs to produce potentially life-threatening hypertensive crises. The

foods most commonly implicated include cheese, chianti, chicken liver, pickled herrings, broad beans and avocado pears. The drugs most commonly implicated include pethidine, sympathetic amines and levodopa. Tricyclic antidepressants and MAOIs may be used synergistically in the treatment of depression.

Q4.16
A = True
B = False
C = True
D = False
E = False

Digoxin is a cardiac glycoside. It delays conduction through the atrioventricular node by increasing vagal activity. It is thought to be a positive inotrope by inhibiting myocardial Na^+-K^+-ATPase. This results in increased intracellular sodium which is then available for exchange with calcium ions, resulting in increased intracellular calcium and increased myocardial contractility. Digoxin should not be used in bradycardia or second-degree heart block. It is contraindicated in Wolff–Parkinson–White syndrome since the resultant atrioventricular block may encourage conduction through the accessory pathways resulting in arrhythmias. Side-effects and toxicity are more common in hypokalaemia, hypercalcaemia and hypomagnesaemia.

Q4.17
A = False
B = False
C = True
D = True
E = False

Metoprolol is a relatively selective β_1-adrenergic antagonist with no intrinsic sympathomimetic activity. It is a negative inotrope, may increase airway resistance, worsen heart block, and block the catecholamine-mediated symptoms of hypoglycaemia. β-blockers have been shown to decrease the risk of sudden death following myocardial infarction. Metoprolol is an effective treatment for the prophylaxis of migraine.

Q4.18
A = False
B = False
C = False
D = True
E = False
Esmolol is a cardioselective β_1-adrenergic antagonist with no intrinsic sympathomimetic activity. Bromocriptine is a dopaminergic agonist, metformin is a biguanide, and clomiphine (not clonidine) is an oestrogen antagonist. Phenoxybenzamine is an α-adrenergic antagonist used mainly in the management of hypertension associated with phaeochromocytoma.

Q4.19
A = True
B = True
C = True
D = False
E = False
First-order kinetics means that the rate of change of the drug's concentration is directly proportional to that concentration; in zero-order kinetics the rate of change of the drug concentration is independent of that concentration. The volume of distribution of a drug represents the relationship between the total amount of the drug in the body and its plasma concentration. If the volume of distribution is greater than the total body water, extensive tissue distribution of the drug is implied. Conversely, if the volume of distribution is less than the total body water, this suggests that the drug is principally confined to the plasma or extracellular fluid. The plasma half-life is defined as the time required for the concentration of a drug in plasma to decline to half of its initial value. Clearance is defined as the volume of distribution multiplied by the rate of drug elimination.

Q4.20
A = True
B = True
C = True
D = True
E = True
Calcium channel blockers prevent the entry of calcium into cardiac and smooth muscle cells during depolarisation. They may therefore interfere with cardiac conduction and with cardiac and smooth muscle contraction. They decrease the excretion of digoxin by the renal tubules, leading to increased plasma digoxin levels. Nimodipine may act to decrease cerebral

vasospasm and subsequent infarction following subarachnoid haemorrhage, thus decreasing mortality.

Q4.21
A = False
B = True
C = False
D = False
E = True

The maximum recommended daily dose of asprin in adults is 4 g. The chief features of salicylate poisoning are: hyperventilation leading to respiratory alkalosis, tinnitus, deafness, vasodilatation, fever and sweating. Coma occurs rarely and indicates severe poisoning. The associated acid–base disturbances are complex. Treatment includes the replacement of fluid losses, and sodium bicarbonate (1.26%) is given to enhance urinary salicylate excretion when the plasma salicylate concentration is greater than 500 mg litre^{-1} (3.6 mmol litre^{-1}) in adults or 350 mg litre^{-1} (2.5 mmol litre^{-1}) in children. Haemodialysis is the treatment of choice for severe salicylate poisoning and should be considered when the plasma salicylate concentration is greater than 700 mg litre^{-1} (5.1 mmol litre^{-1}) or in the presence of severe metabolic acidosis.

Q4.22
A = True
B = False
C = True
D = True
E = False

Phenelzine is a monoamine oxidase inhibitor used in the treatment of depression. It may interact with sympathomimetic amines to produce severe hypertension. This should be treated promptly with a potent antihypertensive agent. Labetolol, an α- and β-blocker, phentolamine, an α-blocker, or diazoxide, a thiazide vasodilator, would all be suitable. Guanethidine may cause an initial increase in the blood pressure due to the release of noradrenaline from nerve terminals. This is followed by a lowering of blood pressure by adrenergic neurone blockade. Methoxamine is an α-agonist and would increase the blood pressure further.

Q4.23

A = False
B = True
C = False
D = False
E = False

Nausea and vomiting occur early following paracetamol overdose. The other features listed do not occur until more than 36 hours following ingestion. As little as 10–15 g (20–30 tablets) or 150 mg kg^{-1} of paracetamol taken within 24 hours may cause severe hepatocellular necrosis and, less frequently, renal tubular necrosis. Liver damage is maximal 3–4 days following ingestion and may lead to encephalopathy, haemorrhage, hypoglycaemia, cerebral oedema and death. Activated charcoal should be given if either 150 mg kg^{-1} or 12 g of paracetamol have been ingested within the preceding hour. Antidotes such as acetylcysteine and methionine protect the liver if given within 10–12 hours of ingestion; acetylcysteine is effective up to and possibly beyond 24 hours. Patients requiring treatment can be identified from a single measurement of the plasma paracetamol concentration, related to the time of ingestion, provided that this time interval is not less than 4 hours; earlier samples may be misleading.

Q4.24

A = False
B = True
C = False
D = False
E = False

Parenteral nutrition has formed an important part of modern intensive care, but is not without complications including line misplacement, fluid overload, hepatic dysfunction, sepsis and electrolyte imbalances. Longterm complications include gallstones, cholestasis and abnormal liver function tests. The solution in a composite bag may have an osmolality of around 1000 mosm litre^{-1} and therefore should be given via a central vein, although peripheral formulations are available. Factors prolonging peripheral cannula life and preventing thrombophlebitis include the use of soft polyurethane paediatric cannulae and the use of feeds of low osmolality and neutral pH. Only nutritional fluids should be given by the dedicated intravenous line.

Daily monitoring should include fluid balance, blood and urinary electrolytes and osmolality, blood sugar, nitrogen balance and haemoglobin. Weekly monitoring should include albumin, full blood count, clotting screen, calcium, magnesium, iron, folate, B$_{12}$, and phosphate levels. Patients with renal failure are not precluded from receiving parental nutrition but careful fluid balance is essential and filtration or dialysis may be necessary.

Q4.25
A = True
B = True
C = True
D = True
E = True
Plasma cholinesterase is found in the plasma, liver, brain, kidney, intestine and pancreas. Its physiological function is unknown, but it hydrolyses a large number of drugs and therefore is much less specific than acetylcholinesterase. Other drugs metabolised include procaine, trimetaphan, propanidid, procainamide, neostigmine, prostigmine, propofol, tacrine, tetracaine and mivacurium.

Q4.26
A = True
B = False
C = True
D = True
E = True
Renal failure will impair the clearance of drugs principally excreted via the kidneys, resulting in increased plasma levels and possible toxicity. Of the drugs listed, warfarin is metabolised in the liver by the mixed function oxidase system; the remainder are excreted to a significant extent via the kidney.

Q4.27
A = False
B = True
C = True
D = True
E = False
After oral administration, most drugs must pass via the gut mucosa, portal system and liver before they may exert a systemic effect. Drugs that exhibit high first-pass metabolism are rapidly cleared by the liver before reaching the systemic circulation and therefore have a low bioavailability. These include morphine, propranolol, glyceryl trinitrate, lignocaine and pethidine.

Q4.28
A = True
B = True
C = True
D = True
E = True

Carbamazepine is an anticonvulsant drug structurally related to the tricyclic antidepressants; it has been used extensively in the management of central pain states including those listed above. It is also useful in the management of manic depression resistant to lithium.

Q4.29
A = True
B = True
C = False
D = True
E = False

Heparin is a highly negatively charged mucopolysaccharide produced by mast cells. Its molecular weight is approximately 15 000 and it is prepared commercially from bovine lung and bovine and porcine intestine. Its anticoagulant activity is reversed by protamine in a ratio of 1000 units heparin to 1 mg protamine.

Vitamin K may be used to reverse the effects of warfarin.

Q4.30
A = False
B = True
C = False
D = False
E = False

Sudden discontinuation of clonidine preoperatively may result in severe rebound hypertension. Tranylcypromine, a monoamine oxidase inhibitor, should be discontinued two weeks before elective surgery. Imipramine, a tricyclic antidepressant, should not be discontinued, nor should prednisolone. The combined oral contraceptive pill should be discontinued before major surgery or leg surgery in order to reduce the risk of deep venous thrombosis (DVT), which is doubled when taking the combined oral contraceptive pill. The progesterone-only contraceptive pill is not associated with any increased risk of DVT.

5. Clinical Measurement

Q5.1 The basic SI units from which all other units are derived include:

A. temperature (degree Celsius)
B. length (metre)
C. luminous intensity (candela)
D. amount of substance (millimole)
E. current (ampere)

Q5.2 The blood/gas partition coefficient:

A. may be defined as the ratio of the amount of substance present in one phase compared with another, the two phases being of equal volume and in equilibrium.
B. is dependent upon temperature
C. is 0.7 for halothane
D. determines the potency of a volatile anaesthetic agent
E. determines the speed of induction of a volatile anaesthetic agent

Q5.3 Placement of a cannula in the radial artery:

A. allows beat-to-beat monitoring of the systolic, diastolic and mean blood pressures
B. registers a higher systolic pressure than in the same cannula in the aortic arch
C. should only be performed following an Allen's test
D. may be associated with a damped trace if a long, narrow connection catheter is used
E. in modern practice is essentially without significant complications

Q5.4 Surface tension:

A. is measured in newtons per metre
B. is due to repulsive forces at an air and liquid interface
C. varies with temperature
D. is increased in the lung by surfactant, thus helping to prevent the alveoli from collapsing
E. may be measured using a visciometer

Q5.5 In relation to microshock:

A. the severity is dependent on the frequency of the current such that the lower the frequency the more severe the shock.
B. 150 µA may cause ventricular fibrillation if delivered directly to the myocardium
C. it is a risk in patients with pacemakers
D. it will result in an associated skin burn at the site of entry of the current
E. the severity is proportional to the current density

Q5.6 A pH of 7.4 is:

A. a hydrogen ion concentration of 40 nmol litre^{-1}
B. a hydrogen ion concentration of $10^{7.4}$ mol^{-1}
C. a measure of the hydrogen ion activity in a liquid
D. dependent on temperature
E. the negative logarithm to the base 10 of the hydrogen ion concentration

Q5.7 During prolonged surgery the core temperature may usefully be monitored in:

A. the nasopharynx
B. the rectum
C. the external auditory canal adjacent to the tympanic membrane
D. the axilla
E. the lower third of the oesophagus

Q5.8 The speed of uptake of an anaesthetic agent from the lung:

A. is directly proportional to its potency
B. is inversely proportional to the blood/gas solubility
C. is proportional to the cardiac output
D. is increased by a high minute ventilation
E. determines the speed of induction

Q5.9 The following statements are correct:

A. one bar is equivalent to $14.5 \, lb/in^2$
B. if Reynold's number is less than 2000 it implies turbulent flow
C. in turbulent flow the flow is inversely proportional to the pressure gradient
D. in laminar flow the flow is proportional to the pressure gradient
E. $10.2 \, cm \, H_2O$ is equivalent to $750 \, mm \, Hg$

Q5.10 With regard to pulse oximetry, inaccuracies in displayed oxygen saturation may occur:

A. if methaemoglobin is present
B. in the presence of peripheral vasoconstriction
C. if the ear is used rather than the finger
D. in patients with cyanide toxicity following an infusion of sodium nitroprusside
E. in the presence of nail polish

Q5.11 The minimum alveolar concentration (MAC):

A. is measured at one atmosphere
B. is a measure of anaesthetic potency
C. decreases with decreasing body temperature
D. the MAC of sevoflurane is maximal in neonates
E. hyponatraemia will reduce the MAC of isoflurane

Q5.12 The following statements are true:

A. at the isobestic point the absorption of light by oxyhaemoglobin and deoxyhaemoglobin are identical
B. the principle behind a cryoprobe is the adiabatic expansion of a compressed gas
C. the piezoelectric effect may be used to measure anaesthetic vapour concentration
D. in gas chromatography the stationary phase is usually a gas such as nitrogen, helium or argon
E. the absorption of infrared light may be used to measure carbon dioxide concentration

Q5.13 The critical pressure is:

A. the pressure above which a gas becomes a vapour
B. the pressure above which a cylinder should not be filled
C. the pressure above which a stoichiometric mixture of gases will not explode
D. two times atmospheric pressure at 20°C
E. the pressure above which oxygen can be stored as a liquid

Q5.14 With regard to osmolality:

A. osmolality is measured in osmol litre^{-1} of solvent
B. the serum osmolality is approximately 290 mosmol litre^{-1}
C. plasma osmolality is predominantly determined by the sodium concentration
D. osmolality may be measured by the depression of the melting point of a liquid
E. in diabetes insipidus the plasma osmolality will rise

Q5.15 The following statements are correct:

A. a 21 steel wire gauge (SWG) needle is larger than a 23 SWG needle
B. a 4 french gauge catheter will have a circumference of 4 mm
C. a 14 SWG cannula will allow the flow of approximately 4 litre min^{-1}
D. a size 6 endotracheal tube has an external diameter of 6 mm
E. the flow through a cannula is determined by the size of the vein it is inserted in rather than the size of the cannula

Q5.16 When discussing solubility:

A. the Ostwald solubility coefficient may be defined as the volume of gas which dissolves in one unit volume of the liquid at a specified temperature
B. the solubility of a gas decreases with increasing temperature
C. the partition coefficient is independent of temperature
D. the Ostwald solubility coefficient is independent of pressure
E. decompression sickness is due to the decreased solubility of nitrogen in the blood when a rapid return from high ambient pressure to atmospheric pressure occurs

Q5.17 Measurement of oxygen in a mixture of gases may be achieved by:

A. the Severinghaus electrode
B. the Clark electrode
C. mass spectrometry
D. a transcutaneous oxygen electrode
E. an infrared analyser

Q5.18 With regard to biological potentials:

A. the amplitude of the ECG is 1–2/mV
B. the EEG is measured in µV
C. the EMG may interfere with the ECG because similar potential differences are involved
D. α-waves on the EEG have a frequency of 25 Hz
E. the frequency of the ECG is between 0.5 and 100 Hz

Q5.19 The following statements are true of exponential processes:

A. the rate of change at any time is proportional to the amount remaining at that time
B. washout curves are exponential processes
C. the time taken to complete an exponential process is infinity
D. the time constant is the time at which the process would have been complete if the initial rate of change had been maintained
E. during the same process the time constant is shorter than the half-life

Q5.20 When discussing the nerve stimulator:

A. the current flowing may be up to 60 mA
B. the frequency of tetanic stimulation is 50 or 100 Hz
C. the train of four has a pulse duration of 200 µs and a frequency of 2 Hz
D. double burst stimulation may more easily detect fade
E. the negative electrode should ideally be placed over the nerve being stimulated

Q5.21 The Doppler effect:

A. is a decrease in the observed frequency of a signal when the signal source approaches the observer and an increase when the source moves away
B. can be used clinically to determine pressure in a column of liquid
C. is used to measure foetal size
D. is used clinically to measure blood flow in peripheral vessels
E. can measure oxygen flow in the aorta

Q5.22 Concerning magnetic resonance imaging:

A. it can be used for biochemical and angiographic studies
B. it is dependent on the rotation of an x-ray source and detector about the patient
C. ECG monitoring of the patient is not vulnerable to interference
D. modern pacemakers are not affected by the magnetic field
E. oxygen cylinders may not be placed near the scanner

Q5.23 Intracranial pressure monitoring:

A. is routinely performed in alcoholic encephalopathy
B. is without significant risk in current practice
C. uses continuous-flow apparatus similar to that used in invasive blood pressure monitoring
D. directly measures cerebral perfusion pressure
E. indicates that mean intracranial pressure is normally 7–15 mm Hg

Q5.24 Concerning cardiac output measurement:

A. in the dye dilution technique, the cardiac output is equal to the amount of dye injected divided by the area under the semi log plot of dye dilution
B. in the thermodilution technique, two peaks are seen in the washout curve, representing recirculation
C. the Fick principle states that the blood flow to an organ in unit time is equal to the amount of marker substance taken up by the organ in unit time divided by the concentration difference of the substance in the vessels supplying and draining the organ
D. approximately 60% of the total cardiac output passes through the descending aorta and can be measured with the oesophageal Doppler
E. the oesophageal Doppler probe is safe to use in all patients

Q5.25 In respiratory function monitoring:

A. the FEV_1/FVC ratio is typically reduced in restrictive pulmonary disease and normal or high in obstructive pulmonary disease
B. the peak expiratory flow rate is a bedside test for restrictive lung disease
C. the residual volume is the volume of gas remaining in the lungs after a normal expiration
D. maximal voluntary ventilation is measured over 30 seconds
E. closing capacity is measured by Fowler's method

Q5.26 When analysing arterial blood/gas tensions:

A. the base excess is the amount of acid required to achieve normal pH at room temperature
B. the anion gap is normally 2–15 mmol litre^{-1}
C. the standard bicarbonate is normally 24–33 mmol litre^{-1}
D. normal values for mixed venous blood are: O_2 6.1 kPa, CO_2 5.3 kPa
E. excess heparin in the blood/gas sampling syringe results in a falsely low pH

27. When observing the jugular venous waveform

A. the 'a' wave corresponds to ventricular contraction
B. the 'v' wave is due to the rise in atrial pressure before tricuspid opening
C. the 'y' descent corresponds to atrial relaxation
D. Cannon waves occur in atrial fibrillation
E. giant 'v' waves are seen in congestive cardiac failure

Q5.28. With regard to the arterial waveform:

A. the pulse pressure is greater in the aorta than in the dorsalis pedis artery
B. the dicrotic notch becomes more apparent in the peripheral arterial tree
C. damping may result from stiff catheter tubing
D. myocardial contractility may be directly measured from the waveform
E. pulsus alternans occurs in left ventricular failure

Answers to Section 5

Q5.1
A = False
B = True
C = True
D = False
E = True

The seven basic SI units are; length (metre), mass (kilogram), time (seconds), current (ampere), temperature (degree Kelvin), luminous intensity (candela), amount of substance (mole). Derived units include Newton, Pascale, Joule, Watt and Hertz.

Q5.2
A = True
B = True
C = False
D = False
E = True

The blood/gas partition coefficient is temperature-dependent, therefore the temperature must be specified. At 37°C, the blood/gas partition coefficient of halothane is 2.3, that of enflurane is 1.9, isoflurane 1.4, sevoflurane 0.69 and desflurane 0.42. As anaesthesia is determined by the alveolar concentration of the volatile agent, the solubility of the agent in blood will determine its uptake and removal from the alveolus by the circulation. Thus a highly soluble agent such as ether (blood/gas partition coefficient 12) will be rapidly transported away in the blood and its alveolar concentration will increase very slowly. This will result in a slower induction of anaesthesia than with a less soluble agent. The potency of a volatile anaesthetic agent is related to its oil/water solubility; this is the basis of the Meyer–Overton theory of anaesthesia.

Q5.3
A = True
B = True
C = False
D = False
E = False

Invasive monitoring of arterial pressure is useful for many reasons including beat-to-beat monitoring of systolic, diastolic and mean pressures. It is not, however, without complications, such as haematoma formation, arterial damage, emboli and bleeding. In Allen's test the patient's hand is clenched into a fist and the radial and ulnar arteries are both occluded by the observer. The patient then relaxes his hand and the observer releases the pressure over the ulna artery; the hand should then flush within 5 seconds indicating a good collateral flow between the radial and ulna arteries. This is not now routinely performed prior to radial artery catheter placement as it does not in fact reliably determine the adequacy of the ulnar collateral circulation. The wave form displayed from an arterial cannula becomes narrower and increases in amplitude in the peripheral arteries; this is due to the change in the diameter of the vessels such that the pressure recorded is higher in the dorsalis pedis artery than in the radial artery, where it is in turn higher than that in the aorta. Damping of the arterial trace may occur if there are air bubbles in the catheter or clots in the cannula. A long catheter will tend to cause resonance of the trace, the best trace being achieved by using a short, wide, stiff-connection catheter.

Q5.4
A = True
B = False
C = True
D = False
E = False

Surface tension is measured in force per unit length, i.e. newtons per metre, and is the result of forces of attraction between molecules on the surface of a liquid. In the lung, surfactant helps to prevent the alveoli from collapsing on expiration by decreasing the surface tension of the fluid lining the alveolus; thus, as the pressure across the alveolar wall rises on expiration, the surface tension decreases and the alveolar radius remains constant (pressure gradient across the wall of a sphere = 2 × tension/radius). Viscosity, not surface tension, is measured with a viscometer.

Q5.5
A = True
B = True
C = True
D = False
E = True

Microshock may occur if a current generated by faulty equipment is delivered directly to the myocardium (e.g. via a central venous cannula or pacemaker). The severity of the shock is dependent on the current density and the frequency, and as little as 100 µA may be sufficient to cause ventricular fibrillation. Timing of the shock is also important (e.g. in the R on T phenomenon, where at the middle of the T-wave the myocardium is vulnerable to the establishment of re-entry arrhythmias). The currents involved in microshock are far too small to cause skin burns.

Q5.6
A = True
B = False
C = True
D = True
E = True

The pH may be defined as the negative logarithm to the base 10 of the hydrogen ion concentration, i.e. pH = $-\log[H^+]$, thus a pH of 7 represents a hydrogen ion concentration of 10^{-7} mol litre^{-1} and a pH of 7.4 is a hydrogen ion concentration of $10^{-7.4}$ mol litre^{-1}. This is the equivalent to a hydrogen ion concentration of 40 nmol litre^{-1}. The normal pH of arterial blood is 7.34–7.46, which corresponds to [H$^+$] of 34–46 nmol litre^{-1}.

Q5.7
A = True
B = True
C = True
D = False
E = True

In man the central core of the body is maintained at a constant temperature ($37 \pm 0.5°C$), while the surface layers may be more variable ($32–35°C$). This central core includes the brain, thoracic and abdominal organs. Monitoring temperature may be achieved by electrical methods (thermocouple, thermistor and platinum resistance wire), or non electrical (liquid thermometers, gas expansion thermometers, bimetallic strips, infrared thermometry). The tympanic membrane correlates closely with brain temperature and has rapid response time, but there is risk of tympanic membrane rupture, and of inaccuracy if excessive ear wax is present. It is important to monitor temperature in the lower third of the oesophagus to avoid cooling by the inspired fresh gas flow. Rectal temperature measurement will have slow response to changes in core temperature due to insulation by faeces. Blood temperature may be monitored directly by thermistor in pulmonary artery catheters. The axillary temperature does not accurately reflect core temperature.

Q5.8
A = False
B = True
C = True
D = True
E = True

The uptake of an anaesthetic agent from the alveolus into the blood stream is dependent upon the concentration gradient between the inspired concentration and the venous concentration, the solubility of the agent in the blood, the pulmonary blood flow, and therefore the cardiac output and the minute ventilation.

Q5.9
A = True
B = False
C = True
D = True
E = False

10.2 cm H_2O = 1 kPa = 7.5 mm Hg. 1 bar = 14.5 lb/in^2 = 100 kPa = 750 mm Hg. Reynold's number is the product of the velocity of the fluid, the density of the fluid and the diameter of the tube, divided by the viscosity of the fluid. If it is greater than about 2000 the flow is likely to be turbulent, and if it is less than 2000 it is likely to be laminar. In turbulent flow, the flow is inversely proportional to the pressure gradient, and to the square roots of the length of the tube and the density of the fluid. During laminar flow, the flow is determined by the Hagen Poiseuille equation:

$$\text{Flow} = \frac{\pi \times \text{pressure gradient} \times \text{radius}^4}{8 \times \text{length} \times \text{viscosity}}$$

Q5.10
A = True
B = True
C = False
D = False
E = True

Pulse oximetry depends on the differential absorption of two different wavelengths of light by oxyhaemoglobin and deoxyhaemoglobin. Although a useful monitor, it may be subject to error in the presence of ambient light penetrating around the protective cover, carboxyhaemoglobin, methaemoglobin and other abnormal haemoglobins, peripheral vasoconstriction, low cardiac output states, movement and pigment on the skin or nails.

Q5.11
A = True
B = True
C = True
D = False
E = True
The minimum alveolar concentration of an anaesthetic is that concentration which if inhaled in 100% oxygen prevents 50% of the population from moving in response to surgical/noxious stimulation. It is inversely related to the anaesthetic potency. The concentration in the alveolus is directly related to the concentration in the central nervous system regardless of uptake and distribution of agent to other tissues. MAC may be reduced by many factors, including decreased atmospheric pressure, decreased body temperature, age (lower in neonates and the elderly), hyponatraemia, opiates, clonidine, and calcium antagonists. It is unaffected by duration of anaesthesia, gender, acidaemia/alkalaemia, hyper/hypocapnoea.

Q5.12
A = True
B = True
C = True
D = False
E = True
The isobestic points for oxygen oximetry are 590 nm and 805 nm, and these may be used as reference points where light absorption is independent of degree of saturation but is solely dependent on the haemoglobin concentration.

The alteration in the state of a gas without allowing it to exchange heat energy with the surroundings is called adiabatic change. Thus, if a gas is compressed without exchanging heat energy with its surroundings, its temperature will rise; indeed a system of cooling may be required to prevent explosion. In the case of a cryoprobe, a compressed gas is allowed rapidly to expand adiabatically resulting in cooling of the probe tip.

If an electric current is applied across a quartz crystal it will contract slightly; this is known as the piezoelectric effect. The crystal may then be coated in oil and made to oscillate at its resonant frequency by an appropriate alternating current. If an anaesthetic agent is then dissolved in the oil it will alter the resonant frequency in proportion to its concentration.

Gas chromatography may be used to separate and identify a mixture of gases. It consists of a stationary phase (e.g. silica–alumina), and a mobile phase (e.g. nitrogen, helium or argon). The gas mixture to be analysed is added to the mobile phase and its constituents pass through the column at a rate dependent upon their relative solubilities between the two phases.

Gases such as carbon dioxide, which have two or more different atoms in their molecules), absorb infrared light in proportion to their partial pressure. This is the basis of capnography.

Q5.13
A = False
B = False
C = False
D = False
E = False

When referring to gases and vapours, the critical pressure is the pressure of a substance at its critical temperature. The critical temperature is the temperature above which a substance cannot be liquefied by pressure alone. Above the critical temperature, and therefore the critical pressure, a substance is described as a gas, and below the critical temperature it is described as a vapour.

Q5.14
A = False
B = True
C = True
D = False
E = True

Osmolality describes the concentration of a solution in terms of osmoles of solute per kilogram of solvent. Osmolarity is the number of osmoles per litre of solution. Osmoles = the molecular weight of a substance divided by the number of freely moving particles liberated in solution. Thus 1 mmol of a salt, which dissolves into two ions, provides two milliosmoles.

The plasma osmolality is normally 280–290 mmol litre^{-1}; this may be measured in the laboratory or calculated from:

Approximate osmolality = 2[Na] + [urea] + [glucose]

In the laboratory, plasma osmolality may be measured by the depression of the freezing point of the liquid below that of water. In diabetes insipidus the plasma osmolality will rise due to the uncontrolled excretion of large volumes of very dilute urine.

# Q5.15
A = True
B = True
C = False
D = False
E = False

A 14 steel wire gauge (SWG) cannula will allow a flow of approximately one litre every four minutes. It is the size of the cannula which determines the flow rate, not the size of vein. The size of an endotracheal tube refers to its internal diameter.

# Q5.16
A = False
B = True
C = False
D = True
E = True

The solubility of a gas is dependent upon temperature, decreasing as the temperature increases. This may be illustrated by heating water: as its temperature rises and it begins to boil, gases come out of solution in the form of bubbles which are released into the atmosphere.

The Ostwald solubility coefficient is measured at a specified temperature and pressure. The partition coefficient, like the Ostwald solubility coefficient, is also dependent upon temperature.

Decompression sickness occurs in divers, and is due to the solubility of nitrogen decreasing as the diver returns too rapidly from the depths to atmospheric pressure, thus the nitrogen comes out of solution as small bubbles in joints and other tissues.

# Q5.17
A = False
B = True
C = True
D = False
E = False

The Severinghaus electrode is used to measure the partial pressure of carbon dioxide in a liquid, usually arterial blood. The Clark electrode is a polargraphic electrode using a platinum cathode and a silver/silver chloride anode. These lie in an electrolyte solution while a voltage is passed between them. The more oxygen present the greater the current flow between the electrodes. A mass spectrometer is used to identify and measure many different compounds including respiratory gases. The infrared analyser is used to measure carbon dioxide in a mixture of gases. The transcutaneous oxygen electrode is used to measure indirectly the arterial partial pressure of oxygen in vivo.

Q5.18
A = True
B = True
C = True
D = False
E = True

The potentials involved in the EEG are much smaller than those of the ECG or EMG, being of the order of approximately 50 μV. Alpha waves occur at 8–13 Hz, beta waves at 18–30 Hz, theta waves at 4–7 Hz, and delta waves at 1–4 Hz. The potentials produced electromyographically range from about 100μV to many mV and therefore they will interfere with the signal received from the ECG. The range of frequencies of the various parts of the ECG is between 0.5 Hz and 100 Hz.

Q5.19
A = True
B = True
C = True
D = True
E = False

As the duration of an exponential process is infinity, the total time cannot be used to measure the duration of the process; therefore the half-life and the time constant are used to describe this. The half-life is the time for the quantity to fall to half of its original value; the time constant is the time at which the process would have been complete had the initial rate of change been maintained. After one time constant the original quantity has fallen to 37% of its original value, thus the time constant is longer than the half-life.

Q5.20
A = True
B = True
C = True
D = True
E = True

Double burst stimulation consists of two short tetanic bursts separated by 750 ms. The duration of each square wave impulse is 200 μs and, although it may vary, there are usually three impulses per burst. The second burst is then compared with the first to assess the degree of residual neuromuscular blockade.

Q5.21

A = False
B = False
C = False
D = True
E = False

The Doppler effect is an increase in the observed frequency of a signal as its source moves towards the observer and a decrease as it moves away. A common example is the sound of a fast-moving passing car. The principle is used clinically to determine velocities and flow rates in moving substances (e.g. the transoesophageal doppler for determining cardiac output, and the obstetric foetal heart rate monitor). Ultrasound is used to assess foetal size but this uses the time taken for the ultrasound wave to travel from the probe back to the sensor to build up a picture of the body. TOE can measure cardiac output by measuring flow in the aorta; it does not measure oxygen delivery.

Q5.22

A = True
B = False
C = False
D = False
E = True

Magnetic Resonance Imaging (MRI) utilises a powerful magnetic field to align atoms in this field. The atoms must have an odd number of protons or neutrons to be affected. Radiofrequency pulses are applied causing deflection of the atoms; when the pulse stops, the atoms return to their previous alignment, emitting energy which is subjected to computer analysis to provide graphical or metabolic information. There are several problems relating to the powerful magnetic field. Ferromagnetic objects will become dangerous projectiles in the magnetic field, and objects such as cylinders, needles and laryngoscope batteries must be kept out of range. Intracranial clips, pacemakers and prosthetic heart valves may also be affected. Metal joint prostheses may be heated by the radiofrequency pulses. Monitoring and resuscitation may also be problematic near the magnetic field. Sedation or anaesthesia may be required by patients undergoing MRI scanning due to the often prolonged scan times in a noisy and cramped environment, although more modern machines are quicker. Computed Axial Tomography (CAT scanning), involves an x-ray source and a detector rotating stepwise, with the patient midway between them.

Q5.23
A = False
B = False
C = False
D = False
E = True

Indications for intracranial pressure monitoring vary between units but include any cause of coma and raised intracranial pressure. Neurosurgical expertise is required for insertion. The procedure is not without risk. The most common risks are infection and bleeding. The position of monitors used may be extradural, subarachnoid, ventricular or intracerebral. The two main types of intracranial pressure monitoring are fibreoptic transducers and fluid-filled catheters.

The devices are flushed rarely, with small volumes (under 0.2 ml) and continuous flow apparatus is not used. The waveform produced resembles an arterial wave and the cerebral perfusion pressure may be calculated from the equation CPP = ICP – MAP (cerebral perfusion pressure = intracranial pressure – mean arterial pressure).

The mean ICP is normally between 7 and 15 mm Hg, 1–2 kPa, in the supine position.

Q5.24
A = True
B = False
C = True
D = False
E = False

Two peaks are seen in the washout curve using dye dilution due to recirculation of dye. Thermodilution techniques are preferred in clinical practice because only one peak is produced and repeat measurements are easier.

Approximately 75% of the total cardiac output passes through the descending aorta, and this proportion is little changed in high-output states. The proportion may decrease by 10% in low-output conditions. There is good correlation between Doppler and thermodilution measurements of cardiac output, although absolute measurements are generally underestimated with Doppler.

The discomfort produced by the Doppler probe makes it suitable only in sedated or ventilated patients, and there is a risk of oesophageal perforation and haemorrhage. Its use is contraindicated in patients with known pharyngeal, oesophageal or gastric pathology. Smaller nasopharyngeal probes are being developed for use in awake patients.

Q5.25
A = False
B = False
C = False
D = False
E = True

In restrictive pulmonary disease, the FEV_1/FVC ratio is typically normal or high, whereas it is reduced in obstructive disease. The peak expiratory flow rate (PEFR) is the maximal rate of air flow during a sudden forced exhalation and is a bedside test used to monitor obstructive lung disease (e.g. asthma and chronic obstructive pulmonary disease). It is typically 450–700 litre min^{-1} in males and 250–500 litre min^{-1} in females, but is highly dependent on patient effort. The residual volume (RV), the volume of gas remaining in the lung after a maximal expiration, is usually about 1.5 litre in the average 70 kg male; and increases in functional residual capacity (FRC) are usually due to increased RV. (*See Fig. 3.1 on page 81.*)

The maximal voluntary ventilation (maximal breathing capacity) is the maximal minute volume of air and is measured over 15 seconds. It is rarely clinically useful as it is very tiring to perform. It is normally about 120–150 litre min^{-1} and equals approximately 35 × FEV_1.

The closing capacity is the lung volume at which the airways begin to collapse; therefore *closing capacity = closing volume + residual volume*. In Fowler's method, a marker gas, e.g. helium (He), is inhaled at the end of maximal expiration followed by the inspiration of air to total lung capacity. The expired [He] concentration is then measured, and at closing capacity there is a sharp rise in [He]. This rise occurs because the helium bolus entered the upper airways while the lower ones were collapsed at residual volume.

Q5.26
A = False
B = False
C = True
D = False
E = True

The base excess/deficit is the amount of acid/base (in mmol) required to restore 1 litre of blood to normal pH at pCO_2 5.3 kPa and body temperature. It is negative in acidosis and positive in alkalosis, and is used to indicate the metabolic component of acid–base disturbances and in the calculation of the dose of acid or base in its treatment.

The anion gap is normally 4–11 mmol litre^{-1} and is the difference between ($[HCO_3^-] + [Cl^-]$) and ($[Na^+] + [K^+]$). It represents the sum of the unmeasured anions (sulphates, phosphates, plasma proteins). When acidosis is due to a loss of base, the anion gap will be normal. When the metabolic acidosis is associated with an increased anion gap it is due to an increase in acid (e.g. ketoacidosis, lactic acidosis, renal failure and poisoning).

The standard bicarbonate is the plasma concentration of bicarbonate when arterial pCO_2 has been corrected to 5.3 kPa with haemoglobin fully saturated and at a temperature of 37°C. This eliminates the respiratory component of the acid–base disturbance.

Normal blood/gas tensions in mixed venous blood are O_2 5.3 kPa and CO_2 6.1 kPa.

Inaccuracy of blood/gas tension measurements may result from excess acidic heparin, bubbles within the sample, inadvertent venous sampling or ongoing metabolism by blood cells.

Q5.27
A = False
B = True
C = False
D = False
E = True

The venous waveform is obtained from the tracing of the central venous pressure. It can be seen, but not felt, in the neck as the jugular venous pressure (JVP). The JVP reflects the blood volume, venous capacitance and right heart function. It directly measures the 'preload' of the heart. The JVP falls during inspiration and rises during expiration and when pressure is applied to the abdomen (Q sign). The venous wave form has waves and descents.

The 'a' wave is due to atrial systole.

The 'c' wave is due to right ventricular filling before tricuspid valve closure.

The 'v' wave is due to the rise in atrial pressure as the right atrium fills before tricuspid opening.

The 'x' descent is due to atrial relaxation and the 'y' descent is due to atrial emptying as the blood enters the ventricle through the tricuspid valve.

Recognised abnormalities of the venous waveform include:
• No 'a' wave in atrial fibrillation
• Enlarged 'a' wave in tricuspid stenosis; stiff right ventricle (e.g. in pulmonary stenosis and pulmonary hypertension).
• Enlarged 'v' wave in tricuspid regurgitation, in cardiac failure.
• Cannon waves (large waves not corresponding to 'a', 'c', or 'v' waves) in complete heart block or junctional arrhythmias.

(See Fig. 3.2 on page 83.)

Q5.28

A = False
B = True
C = False
D = False
E = True

The shape of the arterial waveform changes along the arterial tree with the peak systolic pressure and pulse pressure increasing and the dicrotic notch becoming more apparent more peripherally. Smaller vessels are less compliant, resulting in higher pressure peaks. Abnormal waveforms may reflect disease with a 'collapsing pulse' in aortic regurgitation, bisferiens pulse in mixed aortic valve disease, and pulsus alternans in left ventricular failure. Excessive damping may occur with air bubbles or kinked catheter tubing, whereas excessive resonance will occur with catheter tubing that is too long or too flexible.

Information about the circulation that may be derived from the arterial waveform includes:

- the arterial blood pressure
- stroke volume and cardiac output from the area under the systolic part of the waveform
- myocardial contractility, indicated by dP/dt
- outflow resistance, estimated by the slope of the diastolic delay
- hypovolaemia, suggested by a low dicrotic notch, narrow width of the waveform and large falls in peak pressure with IPPV breaths.

6. Equipment

Q6.1 Cylinders used on an anaesthetic machine:

A. a carbon dioxide cylinder is usually size D
B. a size E oxygen cylinder contains 680 litres at 15°C
C. carbon dioxide cylinders contain a mixture of vapour and liquid
D. the plastic disc on the cylinder neck gives details of its specific contents
E. the valve block of the cylinder contains two protruding pins arranged in a gas-specific pattern

Q6.2 When using a circle system:

A. soda lime absorbs 26 litre of CO_2 per 100 g of absorbent
B. baralyme is more stable but less efficient than soda lime
C. most vaporisers are placed outside the circuit
D. low flow is defined as less than 1 litre min^{-1}
E. nitrogen washout at the start of the anaesthetic means that a potentially hypoxic mixture may be present in the alveoli (if low flows are used)

Q6.3 Accepted guidelines for monitoring the patient during anaesthesia recommend:

A. the continuous presence of a member of the anaesthetic team
B. if a piece of monitoring equipment is not used the reason should be documented
C. temperature monitoring should be used when appropriate
D. when neuromuscular blocking drugs are used, neuromuscular function must be monitored
E. monitoring should always be attached prior to the commencement of anaesthesia

Q6.4 When using spinal cord monitoring during scoliosis surgery:

A. recordings are affected by hypotension
B. if using isoflurane the concentration must be less than 0.5%
C. sensory-evoked potentials can be measured either cortically or spinally
D. fentanyl decreases the amplitude of sensory-evoked potentials
E. only sensory-evoked potentials are measured

Q6.5 The following statements are true of medical gases stored in cylinders:

A. the pressure inside a full oxygen cylinder is 13,700 kPa
B. the pressure registered on a cylinder of nitrous oxide accurately reflects the amount of nitrous oxide remaining
C. in temperate climates the filling ratio for nitrous oxide is 0.9
D. the cylinders are tested every 5 years by subjecting them to a hydraulic pressure of 22,000 kPa
E. the pressure inside a nitrous oxide cylinder is 750 lb/in²

Q6.6 Referring to the infrared analyser:

A. it relies on the principle that gases have two or more different atoms in their molecule which absorb infrared radiation
B. the presence of nitrous oxide potentially makes the measurement of carbon dioxide inaccurate
C. they cannot be used to measure the concentration of volatile agents
D. carboxyhaemoglobin interferes with the measurement of carbon dioxide
E. high blood alcohol levels may render the measurement of anaesthetic gases inaccurate

Q6.7 The following statements are true of anaesthetic breathing circuits:

A. the Mapleson E may only be used on children under 25 kg
B. during spontaneous ventilation the Mapleson A theoretically requires a fresh gas flow equal to the alveolar ventilation to prevent rebreathing
C. the Magill circuit is suitable for children under 20 kg
D. the Humphrey ADE circuit is more efficient than the Magill for spontaneous respiration
E. the parallel Lack circuit has separate inspiratory and expiratory tubes

Q6.8 Heat and moisture exchangers:

A. increase apparatus dead space
B. can act as bacterial filters if they have a pore size of 0.2 microns
C. produce over 60% relative humidity at normal temperatures
D. are contraindicated in children less than 20 kg
E. provide better humidification than ultrasonic nebulisers

Q6.9 Soda lime:

A. consists of approximately 85% calcium carbonate
B. the reaction with carbon dioxide is endothermic
C. can partially regenerate spontaneously
D. is caustic if inhaled
E. the optimum size of the granules is 1.5–8 mm in diameter

Q6.10 The following statements are true of transoesophageal echocardiography:

A. one or more fan-shaped ultrasound beams are produced by one or more transducers within the shaft of the probe
B. it was developed originally by mounting an ultrasound transducer on the distal end of an ordinary gastroscope
C. may be used in the evaluation of an abdominal aortic aneurysm
D. the probe is necessarily encased in a tough, highly durable sheath in order to protect the transducers from damage
E. the Doppler principle is utilised in colour flow imaging

Q6.11 The following statements are true of thromboelastography:

A. the R time (reaction time) is the period from the time when the blood is placed in the analyser until the initiation of fibrin formation
B. bleeding associated with a prolonged R time may be corrected by the administration of fresh frozen plasma
C. the maximum amplitude (MA) of the thromboelastogram may be reduced in the presence of a low platelet count
D. the amplitude of the thromboelastogram after 60 minutes (A_{60}) is a measure of fibrinolysis
E. it may be useful in the evaluation of bleeding following cardiac surgery

Q6.12 The following statements are true of intraoperative cell salvage:

A. the blood must be anticoagulated as soon as it is collected. This may be achieved by the delivery of heparinised saline to the tip of the suction cannula
B. it is not necessary to anticoagulate the blood in the suction tubing as the reservoir contains heparinised saline
C. the red blood cells must be re-suspended in heparinised saline prior to re-infusion into the patient
D. citrate may be used instead of heparin as the anticoagulant
E. no anticoagulation is necessary

Q6.13 The following statements are true of the anaesthetic machine:

A. when checking the machine the gas pipelines should remain connected
B. the emergency oxygen supply delivers up to 10 litres min^{-1}
C. the pressure on the back bar is 400 kPa
D. if the Bodock seal becomes dislodged it is possible to fit a nitrous oxide cylinder to the oxygen yolk
E. the pressure relief valve on the back bar opens at 30–40 kPa

Q6.14 When using methods for non-invasive blood pressure monitoring:

A. the cuff width should be smaller than the diameter of the arm
B. if the cuff is too small the reading will be erroneously low
C. because of the small diameter of a neonate's arm, blood pressure cuffs cannot be used
D. cardiac arrhythmias may render the recorded blood pressure inaccurate
E. automated blood pressure machines measure mean pressure more accurately than systolic pressure

Q6.15 The following is true of Entonox cylinders:

A. the pressure inside is 4400 kPa
B. they should be stored vertically
C. the pseudocritical temperature is −5.5°C
D. they have white shoulders and blue bodies
E. if separation occurs the nitrous oxide will be used up before the oxygen

Q6.16 When considering vaporisers:

A. the TEC 5 vaporiser delivers more volatile agent at very low flow rates than is indicated by the dial setting
B. the portable drawover EMO vaporiser is not temperature-compensated
C. a missing O-ring seal from a vaporiser would result in a leak which would not be detectable on routine check of the anaesthetic machine
D. two vaporisers may be used in sequence in the modern anaesthetic machine
E. desflurane vaporiser needs to be heated to 29°C

Q6.17 The following statements are true of monitoring oxygenation:

A. pulse oximeters use the difference in the transmission of light at wavelengths 660 nm and 940 nm through arterial and venous blood to calculate the oxygen saturation of arterial blood
B. standard pulse oximeters can be used in the MRI scanner but may be unreliable
C. in-line measurement of PaO_2 is possible but only in the research setting, and is not yet accurate enough for clinical use
D. use of a transcutaneous oxygen electrode in neonates requires local warming of the skin and is associated with a risk of burns
E. as the absorption of light by sickle haemoglobin is less than HbA, pulse oximeters tend to under-read the oxygen saturation

Q6.18 The following statements are true of tracheal tubes:

A. the Robertshaw is a double-lumen tube with a carinal hook
B. Z 79- IT marked on PVC tubes refers to the strain of rabbit used for implant testing
C. a Cole tube should not be used for ventilation postoperatively as it causes tracheal damage
D. a Montando tube may be used during a laryngectomy
E. a low-pressure cuff should be inflated to a pressure of 2.5 kPa

Q6.19 When considering the use of airway devices:

A. the LMA is contraindicated in the latex-sensitive patient
B. tracheostomy tubes have a posteriorly-facing bevel
C. when using transtracheal ventilation a cannula of at least 16 SWG is required
D. the Combitube is a single-lumen tube with two cuffs, one tracheal and one oesophageal
E. a tracheal tube used to pass blindly through an intubating LMA must be 6mm or less

Q6.20 The following statements are correct with regard to operating department pollution:

A. activated charcoal can be used for scavenging volatile agents
B. using low-flow systems avoids the need of a scavenging system
C. the recommended maximum exposure limit for nitrous oxide is 10 parts per million in any 8-hour period
D. air in theatre should be changed 15 times per hour
E. pollution is greatest when using a T-piece as it is impossible to scavenge expired gases

Q6.21 When monitoring a patient during anaesthesia:

A. awareness may occur in up to 1% of patients during balanced anaesthesia
B. bispectral analysis allows depth of anaesthesia to be checked
C. a BIS recording of 50 is compatible with normal sleep
D. BIS recordings are affected by opiate levels
E. the isolated forearm technique identifies conscious awareness

Answers to Section 6

Q6.1
A = False
B = True
C = True
D = False
E = False

Medical gas cylinders are made in various sizes. A is the smallest and J the largest. Most cylinders attached to anaesthetic machines are size E; however, the smaller, size C CO_2 cylinders are used but should not be left attached to the anaesthetic machine. If attached they are not to be left switched on. Oxygen and air cylinders contain only gas; CO_2 and nitrous oxide cylinders contain a mixture of vapour and liquid. The disc on the neck indicates the year when the cylinder was last checked. The cylinder valve block contains two holes into which the pins on the yolk locate to ensure correct attachment of the cylinders.

Q6.2
A = True
B = True
C = True
D = True
E = True

All circle systems require an efficient CO_2 absorber in the circuit. Soda lime contains calcium, sodium and potassium hydroxide with silica, and baralyme contains calcium and barium hydroxide. Baralyme is denser and approximately 15% less efficient than soda lime.

Vaporisers can be placed inside or outside the circuit. However, most are placed on the back bar of the machine and outside the circle itself. As nitrogen in the alveolar air is washed out at the beginning of an anaesthetic it is usual to use higher fresh gas flows at the start to prevent alveolar hypoxia and then decrease flows to below 1 litre min^{-1} as the case continues.

Q6.3

A = False
B = True
C = True
D = False
E = False

The Association of Anaesthetists of Great Britain and Ireland published 'Recommendations for Standards of Monitoring During Anaesthesia and Recovery' in December 2000.

The requirement is for the continuous presence of the anaesthetist. Use and non-use of routine equipment must always be documented; if equipment malfunctions this should be recorded; and if anaesthetia is undertaken without particular monitoring equipment the reason for continuing should be documented. Monitoring should be attached before the induction of anaesthesia if possible; however, it is accepted that in young children and some developmentally-delayed adults this is not feasible. Monitoring should always be attached as soon as possible during induction. Neuromuscular function monitors must always be *available* if relaxants are used.

Q6.4

A = True
B = False
C = True
D = True
E = False

It is important that as many factors as possible are kept stable during spinal cord monitoring, and that any physiological or pharmacological changes are reported to the neurophysiologist doing the monitoring. Factors known to affect the recording include hypotension, hypothermia, changes in level of anaesthesia and difficulties with positioning of the patient. Potentials are recorded from motor and sensory modalities and are usually recorded either via scalp electrodes, recordings from muscles, or direct recording via an epidural catheter sensor.

Increasing levels of inhalational agent may decrease the amplitude of sensory potentials in particular, but constant concentrations of isoflurane 0.5%–1% are suitable. Fentanyl in higher doses will decrease the amplitude of sensory potentials but has minimal effect on motor potentials. Any acute changes in the recordings must be reported to the surgeon so they make adjustments to the local cord stresses, and so damage to the cord is avoided whenever possible.

Q6.5
A = True
B = False
C = False
D = True
E = True

Nitrous oxide and carbon dioxide are stored as a mixture of vapour and liquid within the cylinder. The filling ratio for both nitrous oxide and carbon dioxide is 0.75 in temperate areas and is slightly lower, 0.67, in hot climates. The filling ratio is the weight of nitrous oxide with which the cylinder is actually filled divided by the weight of water the cylinder could hold. Therefore it is not until all the liquid has been used up that the pressure exerted by the nitrous oxide vapour will begin to fall, i.e. when the cylinder is almost empty. It is therefore more appropriate to determine the contents of liquid-containing cylinders by weight rather than pressure. The pressure in a nitrous oxide cylinder is 50 kPa × 100, i.e. 750 lb in^{-1}.

Q6.6
A = True
B = True
C = False
D = False
E = True

Gases with two or more different atoms absorb infrared radiation and the amount absorbed is proportional to the amount of gas present. Infrared analysers measure carbon dioxide, nitrous oxide and inhalational anaesthetic agents. Water vapour must be removed, as it is a potent absorber of infrared light. Collision broadening may occur in which some of the energy absorbed by the carbon dioxide molecules is transferred on collision to the nitrous oxide molecules, thus allowing the carbon dioxide to absorb more infrared radiation. This may result in inaccuracies in the carbon dioxide concentration measured and a correction factor is used within the analyser.

Q6.7
A = False
B = True
C = False
D = True
E = True

Mapelson classified anaesthetic breathing systems into A (Magill, Lack, parallel Lack), B, C, D (Bain) and E (Ayre's T-piece). In terms of fresh gas flow required to prevent rebreathing, the Mapleson A is the most efficient for spontaneous respiration, and the Mapelson D is most efficient for assisted ventilation. A system with a pressure-limiting valve (Mapleson A–D), in children less than 25 kg, increases the work of breathing. However, the Ayre's T-piece can be used in patients over 25 kg provided that the reservoir limb has a diameter sufficient to produce less than 2 cm H_2O resistance and a volume approximately the same as the patient's tidal volume.

The Humphrey ADE is a hybrid system which can function in A or E mode depending on the position of a lever; it is a very efficient system. The Lack coaxial system (Bain) has the inspiratory gases going through the outer tube and expiratory ones via an inner tube; thus, if the inner tube fractures, inspiratory and expiratory gases mix causing rebreathing. The parallel Lack separates the inspiratory and expiratory tubes so this problem does not occur.

Q6.8
A = True
B = True
C = True
D = False
E = False

Heat and moisture exchangers (HMEs) are the most common humidifiers in use. They are light, efficient and inexpensive. However, they do add to equipment dead space and to the resistance of breathing. This becomes more important in smaller patients. However, HMEs are designed for use in babies less than 10 kg. An HME will produce 60%–70% humidity in normal working temperatures but a high frequency ultrasonic nebuliser will add far more water droplets to the gases. These are very efficient but they are expensive and may result in excess water being deposited in the airway.

Q6.9
A = False
B = False
C = True
D = True
E = True

Soda lime consists of approximately 94% calcium hydroxide, 5% sodium hydroxide, 1% potassium hydroxide and silica.

The reaction between carbon dioxide and soda lime requires water and is exothermic; the products are calcium carbonate and water. Some regeneration after exhaustion can occur spontaneously. Soda lime, if inhaled, can cause respiratory tract burns.

Q6.10
A = False
B = True
C = False
D = False
E = True

Transoesophageal echocardiography is a useful investigative and monitoring tool, which is becoming increasingly available in the operating theatre. The original transoesophageal echocardiography probe was developed by mounting a single ultrasound transducer on the tip of a gastroscope. However, most probes now have two transducers arranged at right angles in the tip (not the shaft) of a purpose-built instrument. Transoesophageal echocardiography may be used to evaluate intrathoracic structures below the level of the carina. Although limited views of the liver may be obtained, it is not possible to gain clinically useful information about the abdominal aorta. Although the echocardiography machine is relatively durable, the actual transoesophageal probe is delicate and requires great care during use and storage.

Colour flow imaging is a form of pulsed Doppler imaging. The transducer emits pulses of ultrasound at a known frequency. These hit red blood cells within the heart or vasculature and are reflected back to the probe at a different frequency depending upon the velocity of the red blood cells. By convention, different colours are ascribed according to the direction of flow, (red indicates flow towards the transducer, blue indicates flow away from the transducer) and the velocity of the flow is indicated by the brightness of the colour.

Q6.11
A = True
B = True
C = True
D = True
E = True

The thromboelastogram measures the development, magnitude and maintenance of the sheer strength of a clot. The coagulation profile may then be qualitatively or quantitatively analysed (with the aid of computer software) in order to determine if there is a normal, hypo or hypercoagulable state. In the evaluation of the thromboelastogram, five parameters of clot formation are analysed. The R time is the latent period from the time when the blood is placed in the cup until initial fibrin formation. The K time is a measure of the time for the developing clot to reach a particular strength. The α angle represents the speed of fibrin cross linking i.e. clot strengthening. The MA (maximum amplitude) represents the ultimate strength of the clot, and the

A_{60} is the rate of decline of the maximum amplitude of the trace after 60 minutes and represents clot lysis. Broadly speaking the R time is increased in factor deficiency, anticoagulation and severe thrombocytopenia, the K time is increased in factor deficiency and thrombocytopenia, the α angle is decreased in hypofibrinogenaemia, the MA is decreased in thrombocytopenia and the A_{60} is increased in fibrinolysis.

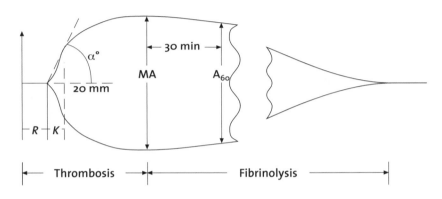

Fig. 6.1: Thromboelastogram trace

Q6.12
A = True
B = False
C = False
D = True
C = False

Intraoperative cell salvage involves the collection and immediate anticoagulation of shed blood; this may then be processed and the red blood cells, or less frequently the unwashed blood, is re-infused into the patient. Anticoagulation is achieved by a solution of heparin or citrate in normal saline which is delivered near to the tip of the suction cannula; thus the blood is mixed with anticoagulant immediately it is aspirated from the wound. The collection reservoir also contains some anticoagulant solution. Following processing, the washed red blood cells are re-suspended in normal saline prior to re-infusion into the patient.

Q6.13

A = True
B = False
C = True
D = False
E = True

AAGBI guidelines now recommend that the machine should not be disconnected but that the tug test should be applied to the pipelines.

The emergency oxygen supply should provide between 35 litre min^{-1}
and 75 litre min^{-1} flow. Anaesthetic machines work at a pressure of
300–400 kPa. As the pressure in a full oxygen cylinder is 13 700 kPa it
needs to pass through pressure-reducing valves before reaching the
patient. Pipeline pressure is 405 kPa, so reducing valves are not required;
however, flow restrictors are used in the machine to protect the flowmeters from pipeline pressure when the pipelines are connected. The
flowmeters act to decrease the pressure in the back bar to just above
atmospheric for clinical use. It is the pin index system that ensures that it
is impossible to attach the wrong cylinder to the yolk. The Bodock seal
ensures a tight gas seal between the cylinder and the yolk. The pressure
relief valve prevents damage to the machine should there be a build-up of
pressure due to an occlusion. Separate pressure-limiting valves are inte-
grated into the breathing system which limit the pressure there to 6–8 kPa.
This protects the patient from excess pressure and barotrauma.

Q6.14

A = False
B = False
C = False
D = True
E = False

An appropriate cuff width is approximately 120% of the diameter of the
arm. Use of smaller cuffs will result in an erroneously high pressure recording. A wide selection of small cuff sizes is available for use in babies.
Automated blood pressure machines use a transducer to detect the return of
flow to the arm following cuff inflation. Thus the systolic pressure is most
accurately measured, while diastolic and mean pressures are less reliably
measured by this method.

# Q6.15
A = False
B = False
C = True
D = False
E = False

The pressure inside the Entonox cylinder is the same as in an oxygen cylinder, namely 13 700 kPa. The cylinders have blue and white shoulders and a blue body, and should be stored horizontally above 0°C to avoid separation of the two gases. The pseudocritical temperature is the temperature below which the mixture of gases separates out into its constituent parts. If separation occurs in an Entonox cylinder, oxygen is used up first, leading to the delivery of a hypoxic mixture as the cylinder empties.

# Q6.16
A = True
B = False
C = False
D = False
E = False

The TEC (SelectaTec) vaporiser series has evolved continuously since its development in 1972. TEC vaporisers are temperature-compensated, and the output of a TEC 5 vaporiser is less affected by the fresh gas flow than earlier models. However, it still delivers slightly more volatile agent at very low FGF rates than is indicated on the dial. Portable vaporisers such as the EMO (Epstein–Mackintosh–Oxford), although using air and additional oxygen drawn over the volatile agent, are thermo-compensated. When checking the anaesthetic machine, correct mounting of the vaporiser is routinely checked by using a flow of 5 litre min^{-1} of oxygen and occluding the common gas outlet, noting depression of the rotameter bobbin as the back pressure rises. Leaks from the vaporiser, and subsequent incorrect delivery of adequate anaesthetic concentrations, are a cause of awareness during anaesthesia. When more than one vaporiser is mounted on the back bar a pushrod system prevents them from both being turned on at the same time. Because the boiling point of desflurane is approximately room temperature (23°C) the TEC 6 desflurane vaporiser has been developed which has an electrical supply to heat the vaporiser chamber to 39°C, thus ensuring complete vaporisation of the liquid desflurane which then passes to the outlet to mix with the FGF. Pressure transducers monitor and adjust the vaporiser to ensure reliable vapour delivery. Internal switches cut out the system if the temperature exceeds 57°C or if the vaporiser becomes tilted or empty.

Q6.17
A = True
B = False
C = False
D = True
E = False

The wavelengths of light red (660 nm) and infrared (940 nm) are absorbed differently by arterial and venous blood. The pulse oximeter bombards the tissues with these many times per second and calculates the ratio of the difference in their absorption. It is difficult to establish satisfactory monitoring in the MRI scanner. However, specialised fiberoptic pulse oximeters are available. These are not affected by the magnet, which can induce electrical current and heat in standard cabling. Use of standard pulse oximeters is associated with skin burns and inadequate quality of recordings. In-line monitoring has become increasingly available and is in clinical use, especially in the ICU and cardiac anaesthesia and on bypass machines. Transcutaneous oxygen electrodes contain a heater which warms the skin locally to 42°C. This causes the blood vessels to dilate so that oxygen used by the skin is negligible compared to the amount in the capillaries and thus the skin and capillary oxygen tension approximates to the arterial oxygen tension. The probes must be moved regularly to avoid skin burns. If the thermistor controlling the output of the heater fails, the skin temperature may rise excessively and burns may occur.

Although there are differences in the absorption patterns of various haemoglobin types, these are small and do not usually affect the accuracy of pulse oximetry. Certain rare haemoglobin types, including Hammersmith and Koln haemoglobin, or the presence of carboxyhaemoglobin or methaemoglobin, will produce inaccuracies in the recording of haemoglobin oxygen saturation.

Q6.18
A = False
B = False
C = False
D = True
E = True

The Robertshaw is a double-lumen red rubber tube used for thoracic anaesthesia. Unlike the Carlens tube it does not have a carinal hook. Z 79 refers to the room in which the Committee on Anesthesia Equipment of the USA Standards Institute met. Cole tubes are used on some neonatal units for longterm ventilation. They have a narrow translaryngeal portion but a widened intraoral portion. The shoulder between these respective areas is designed to make intubation easier in small babies and to prevent inadvertent bronchial intubation. All tracheal tubes are associated with some local mucosal damage. A Cole tube may cause laryngeal damage but is unlikely to cause tracheal damage. A Montando tube has an acute curvature near the tip of the tube for insertion into the trachea during laryngectomy. It is also sometimes used for perioperative ventilation in patients with an established tracheostomy. Tracheal cuffs allow a seal in the trachea, so permitting ventilation without a leak and preventing the aspiration of pharyngeal or gastric contents. The low-pressure, high-volume cuffs allow a larger area of mucosal contact than the high-pressure cuff, which means there is less reduction in the mucosal blood flow and ischaemic damage is less likely.

Q6.19

A = False
B = False
C = True
D = False
E = False

LMAs and polyvinylchloride (PVC) tracheal tubes are all safe in the latex-allergic patient. Many designs are available for tracheostomy tubes. They tend to be short, acutely angled, with a non-bevelled end, as the distance from the tracheal stoma and the carina in the adult is variable and may be short.

The Combitube is designed for use in the management of the difficult airway or in the trauma or arrest situation. It is a double-lumen tube and has two cuffs. It can be positioned either in the oesophagus or in the trachea. If it is in the trachea then the lungs are ventilated via the patent tracheal lumen. However, if it is positioned in the oesophagus ventilation is achieved via perforations in the pharyngeal portion of the blind-ending oesophageal lumen.

A 6mm tracheal tube is the largest that will reliably pass through a standard LMA. The intubating LMA will allow passage of a 9 mm tube.

Q6.20

A = True
B = False
C = False
D = True
E = False

Scavenging of anaesthetic gases and volatile agents is essential in all locations. COSHH (the Control of Substances Hazardous to Health) regulations advise limits of 100ppm for nitrous oxide, isoflurane 50 ppm and halothane 10 ppm. COSHH came into force in 1989 and the regulations were revised in 1994. Scavenging systems can be attached to the expiratory limb of the

T-piece to allow efficient scavenging. Pollution is greater in paediatric practice due to the number of gas inductions and the likelihood of gas escape during these inductions.

Q6.21

A = False
B = True
C = True
D = False
E = True

Some form of awareness may occur in approximately 3 in 1000 anaesthetisations. Awareness is usually related either to poor anaesthetic technique or equipment failure. Memory for intraoperative events can be explicit, i.e. there is consciousness and explicit learning, or implicit, i.e. there is unconsciousness but implicit learning. Clinical signs of the depth of anaesthesia can be inaccurate in identifying awareness. Methods of assessing depth of anaesthesia are: clinical, EEG, evoked potentials, oesophageal contractility and EMG. The conventional EEG is bulky and difficult to interpret; the cerebral function monitor is easier to read but less informative. The BIS monitor (power spectral analysis) is a graphical display of complicated data and is easier to read than the EEG. The Bispectral Index Scale, which uses computerised analysis of the EEG, employs the variables frequency, band power, band frequency and spectral edge frequency. The BIS score is from 0 to 100 where 0 = complete lack of cortical activity and 100 = fully awake. Using the bispectral analysis of the ECG, change in the depth of anaesthesia is reflected in the BIS score where scores of 50–60 are related to an adequate level of anaesthesia. However, scores of 50 have been documented during normal sleep in normal individuals. Opiates, even in high doses, either alone or with nitrous oxide, are not able to prevent awareness. The addition of adequate concentrations of an inhalational agent is important.

7. Medicine

Q7.1 In infective endocarditis:

A. *Streptococcus viridans* endocarditis only occurs in patients with teeth
B. the murmur is characteristically mid-diastolic
C. there must have been a previously abnormal valve
D. in intravenous drug abusers the valve most commonly affected is the pulmonary valve
E. Osler's nodes are pathognomonic

Q7.2 The following statements are true in haemophilia A:

A. haemarthrosis may occur
B. the skin bleeding time is characteristically prolonged
C. the partial thromboplastin time is prolonged
D. it is only clinically important in males
E. spontaneous bleeding into the skin results in purpura

Q7.3 A symmetrical peripheral neuropathy is typical of:

A. vitamin deficiency
B. carpal tunnel syndrome
C. poliomyelitis
D. carcinoma of the bronchus
E. multiple sclerosis

Q7.4 Following a massive pulmonary embolus:

A. the left atrial pressure rises
B. the right atrial pressure rises
C. the central venous pressure decreases with falling cardiac output
D. pulsus paradoxus occurs
E. treatment may include a precordial thump

Q7.5   Wasting of the tongue may occur in:

A. motor neurone disease
B. syringobulbia
C. Parkinson's disease
D. pseudobulbar palsy
E. cerebrovascular accident

Q7.6   Primary hyperparathyroidism may present with:

A. renal stones
B. abdominal pain
C. increased absorption and decreased excretion of calcium
D. bone cysts
E. gallstones

Q7.7   The following are consistent with a diagnosis of carcinoma of the bronchus:

A. hypertrophic pulmonary osteoarthropathy
B. hypercalcaemia
C. inappropriate antidiuretic hormone secretion syndrome
D. thrombophlebitis migrans
E. normal pulmonary function

Q7.8   Acute pericarditis may be associated with the following:

A. uraemia
B. sclerosing cholangitis
C. myxoedema
D. rheumatic fever
E. Coxsackie virus infection

Q7.9   Clubbing may be associated with:

A. chronic bronchitis
B. Crohn's disease
C. congenital heart disease
D. bronchiectasis
E. liver abcess

Q7.10 Ulcerative colitis may be complicated by:

A. sclerosing cholangitis
B. malignant change in the affected bowel
C. iritis
D. erythema nodosum
E. stricture formation

Q7.11 The diagnosis of thyrotoxicosis in a young woman may be supported by finding:

A. a goitre
B. enophthalmos
C. menorrhagia
D. pretibial myxoedema
E. sensitivity to the cold

Q7.12 The following statements are true:

A. untreated iron deficiency anaemia is associated with an increased reticulocyte count
B. in sickle cell trait, sickling of the red cells may occur if the patient is exposed to severe hypoxia
C. pernicious anaemia is usually associated with macrocytosis
D. hereditary spherocytosis is a disease in which the red cell surface area is reduced
E   polycythaemia rubra vera is associated with a risk of acute haemolytic crisis

Q7.13 The following statements are true of cystic fibrosis:

A. it is a sex-linked recessive disorder with an incidence of 1 in 2000 births
B. diagnosis may be confirmed by a high sodium concentration in the sweat
C. heterozygotes have a moderately increased susceptibility to chest infections and should receive vaccination against influenza in the winter
D. the lungs are structurally normal at birth
E. approximately 5% of older patients develop cirrhosis

Q7.14 Features of chronic renal failure include:

A. a microcytic hypochromic anaemia
B. hypertension
C. platelet dysfunction
D. a yellow, itchy skin
E. osteoporosis

Q7.15 Plummer–Vinson syndrome is associated with:

A. iron deficiency anaemia
B. female sex
C. pharyngeal pouch
D. dysphagia
E. achalasia of the cardia

Q7.16 Type 1 diabetes mellitus may present with:

A. insidious weight gain
B. hypoglycaemic coma
C. necrobiosis lipoidica
D. polydipsia
E. urinary tract infection

Q7.17 The following statements are true of carcinoid syndrome:

A. the primary tumour is usually in the liver
B. attacks are characterised by flushing, nausea, diarrhoea and
   bronchospasm
C. the syndrome only occurs after the tumour has metastasised
D. urinary vanillyl mandelic acid (VMA) is raised
E. severe paroxysmal hypertension may occur

Q7.18 The following statements are true of the ECG:

A. bundle branch block is present if the QRS complex is greater than 0.12
   seconds wide
B. the QT interval may be prolonged in hypocalcaemia
C. left bundle branch block is characterised by an RSR pattern in V1
D. a bifid P wave is indicative of right atrial hypertrophy
E. hypokalaemia is associated with peaked T waves

Q7.19 Recognised clinical manifestations of Addison's disease include:

A. buccal pigmentation
B. hypertension
C. proximal myopathy
D. an association with autoimmune disease
E. hyponatraemia and hyperkalaemia

Q7.20 The following statements are true of Fallot's tetralogy:

A. it usually presents immediately after birth with severe cardiac failure
B. the femoral pulses are characteristically weak
C. there is a right ventricular outflow tract obstruction
D. central cyanosis is present
E. squatting is characteristic

Q7.21 In a patient with rheumatoid arthritis:

A. carpal tunnel syndrome is common
B. the presence of pulmonary nodules may result in obstructive lung disease
C. alantoaxial subluxation may cause compression of the carotid artery
D. mouth opening may be limited because of trismus
E. there may be associated renal and hepatic abnormalities

Q7.22 In the patient with chronic renal failure:

A. the associated anaemia is normochromic normocytic
B. morphine metabolites may accumulate but are rarely active
C. hypercalcaemia is common
D. there is an increased effect of protein-bound drugs
E. epidural anaesthesia is safer than general anaesthesia

Q7.23 Morbid obesity is associated with:

A. a body mass index of 25
B. increasing morbidity once the body mass index is greater than 22
C. a risk of regurgitation of gastric contents greater than that of the pregnant female
D. glucose intolerance
E. an increased risk of anaphylaxis

Q7.24 In myasthenia gravis:

A. marked painful fasciculations occur with suxamethonium
B. there may be an associated thymic tumour
C. atracurium is the relaxant of choice
D. hypokalaemia is associated with worsening symptoms
E. there may be an associated bronchial tumour

Q7.25 With regard to variant Creutzfeldt-Jacob disease (vCJD):

A. it is caused by the same infective agent as bovine spongiform encephalopathy
B. the disease tends to affect the young
C. high concentrations of the infective agent are found in spinal cord, bone and blood
D. it has transferred from scrapie in cattle
E. it is essential that all surgical equipment is 'single-use' to avoid spread of the disease

Q7.26 With regard to viral infections:

A. the risk of human immunodeficiency virus (HIV) seroconversion following a needle-stick injury is less than 0.5%
B. 10% of patients with Hepatitis B infection will have persistent surface antigen present six months after infection
C. seroconversion following accidental needle-stick injury with hepatitis B is less common than with HIV
D. HIV infection is frequently covert
E. hepatitis C infection can be transferred by contaminated breathing circuits

Q7.27 Complications associated with patients undergoing a treatment for neoplastic disease include:

A. the development of pulmonary complications, when treated with additional oxygen, if taking bleomycin
B. cardiac arrhythmias during methotrexate therapy
C. cardiomyopathy if taking doxorubicin
D. myocardial fibrosis and conduction defects following thoracic irradiation
E. acute renal failure early in treatment of acute lymphocytic leukaemia (ALL)

Q7.28 In the adult patient with longstanding diabetes:

A. poor diabetic control is associated with retrolental fibroplasias and blindness
B. orthostatic hypotension may occur due to sympathetic overactivity
C. silent myocardial ischaemia is more common than in the general population
D. type 2 diabetes usually requires both diet and insulin management
E. hyperosmolar coma is always associated with increased blood ketone levels

Q7.29 In the patient with liver disease:

A. features of end-stage failure include jaundice, encephalopathy and ascites
B. mortality of fulminant liver failure can be up to 90%
C. early death in paracetamol poisoning is usually due to hepatorenal syndrome
D. in alcoholic liver disease, transplantation is contraindicated
E. one-year survival after liver transplantation is around 25%

Q7.30 When considering disturbances in magnesium homeostasis:

A. alcohol withdrawal may precipitate hypermagnesaemia
B. hypomagnesaemia may occur with diuretic use
C. hypomagnesaemia results in neuronal irritability, muscle spasms and tetany
D. hypermagnesaemia may result in heart block and cardiac arrest
E. hypermagneaemia increases the risk of digitalis toxicity

Q7.31 The following statements are true of the risk of thromboembolic disease:

A. The risk is increased with age > 65
B. it is more common in patients with sickle cell disease
C. it occurs in 40%–70% of patients after total hip replacement
D. it may result in fatal pulmonary embolism in 1% of high-risk patients
E. there is an increased risk if factor V Leiden is present

Q7.32 In the patient with an abnormal blood film:

A. Bence Jones proteinuria occurs in approximately 50% of patients with multiple myeloma
B. Howell–Jolly bodies are seen in the peripheral film following splenectomy
C. Acute lymphocytic leukaemia occurs mainly in the elderly
D. Chronic lymphocytic leukaemia is associated with the presence of the Philadelphia chromosome
E. Hodgkin's disease is characteristically associated with impairment of platelet function

Answers to Section 7

Q7.1
A = False
B = False
C = False
D = False
E = True

Infective endocarditis is most commonly caused by *Streptococcus viridans* (45% of all cases), and the most usual, but not exclusive, source is the teeth. In 50% of cases normal healthy valves are affected, and in intravenous drug abusers it is the tricuspid valve which is most commonly involved. The illness may progress rapidly or slowly, but if untreated will result in death. Features include fever, weakness, weight loss, arthralgia, murmurs, anaemia, splenomegaly, mucocutaneous petechiae, and haematuria. Emboli may occur, resulting in sudden effects such as hemiplegia or blindness.

Characteristically the murmur is changing and the patient should be examined every day. Osler's nodes are characteristic and represent immune complex emboli producing hard painful swellings in the fingers, toes, palms and soles.

Q7.2
A = True
B = False
C = True
D = False
E = False

Haemophilia A is a sex-linked recessive condition due to a deficiency in factor VIII, the antihaemophiliac factor. It occurs almost exclusively in males and the female is the carrier. Female carriers may, however, have significantly reduced factor VIII levels which are sometimes low enough to cause bleeding symptoms. All potential or obligate carriers should have their factor VIII assayed before surgery.

Haemophilia is characterised by bleeding, either spontaneously or as a result of trauma, into muscles, joints and internal organs such as the kidney.

The partial thromboplastin time measures the activity of the intrinsic clotting system, i.e. deficiencies in factors V, VIII, IX, X, XI and XII, prothrombin and fibrinogen; it is therefore prolonged in haemophilia.

The prothrombin time measures the activity of the extrinsic clotting system, i.e. deficiencies of factors V, VII, X, prothrombin and fibrinogen, and is therefore normal in haemophilia.

A petechial rash is indicative of platelet dysfunction, not of haemophilia. The skin bleeding time assesses vascular disorders and abnormalities of platelet number and function; it is classically normal in haemophilia. It may be measured by applying a sphygmomanometer cuff to the arm and inflating it to 40 mm Hg. Two standard lancet cuts 1mm deep and 1cm long are made in the skin of the forearm. Bleeding usually stops within 3–8 minutes.

Factor VIII is given preoperatively to haemophiliacs, and then factor VIII levels are measured before surgery. Factor VIII is available either as a concentrate or as recombitant factor VIII. Haemophiliacs should not be treated prior to surgery without advice from the Haemophilia Centre.

Q7.3
A = True
B = False
C = False
D = True
E = False

A peripheral neuropathy is a disorder of peripheral sensory, motor or mixed nerves. It is usually symmetrical and common causes include diabetes mellitus, carcinomatous neuropathy, vitamin B deficiency and drugs such as isoniazid and phenytoin. Rarer causes include uraemia, myxoedema, polyarteritis nodosa, amyloidosis and heavy metal poisoning.

Q7.4
A = False
B = True
C = False
D = False
E = True

A massive pulmonary embolus may present with severe central chest pain, tachypnoea and tachycardia. The cardiac output is reduced by the resultant right ventricular outflow tract obstruction, and therefore the left atrial pressure will fall and the right atrial and central venous pressure will rise. If cardiac arrest occurs, a precordial thump and cardiac massage may help to break up thrombus and reduce the obstruction to the blood flow. This management is recommended in a witnessed cardiac arrest in adults, as it may help to move the embolus more peripherally, sufficiently restoring perfusion. Pulsus paradoxus occurs when the pulse volume decreases excessively on inspiration. This may occur in cardiac tamponade, constrictive pericarditis and severe chronic bronchitis and asthma.

Q7.5
A = True
B = True
C = False
D = False
E = False

Motor neurone disease is characterised by a progressive degeneration of motor neurones in the spinal cord, the motor nuclei of the cranial nerves and within the cerebral cortex. This results in both upper and lower motor neurone signs with sparing of the sensory system. The progressive bulbar palsy results in a wasted, fasciculating tongue which, in combination with wasting of the laryngeal and pharyngeal muscles, results in difficulties with eating and swallowing. In pseudobulbar palsy, although the muscles are weakened they do not show atrophy or fasciculation. Syringobulbia occurs when an expanding cavity of a syringomyelia extends from the foramen magnum into the brain stem. It is characterised by atrophy and fasciculation of the tongue, nystagmus, Horner's syndrome, deafness and impaired facial sensation. Although dysarthria may occur in Parkinson's disease, this is due to a combination of akinesia, tremor and rigidity and not to wasting. The signs of a stroke or cerebrovascular accident are those of an upper motor neurone lesion.

Q7.6
A = True
B = True
C = True
D = True
E = False

Excess secretion of parathyroid hormone results in increased calcium absorbtion from the gut, decreased clearance by the kidney and increased mobilisation from bone. It also increases renal phosphate clearance. The resultant hypercalcaemia may present with bony cysts, peptic ulceration, renal stones and psychiatric disorders (bones, stones, moans and abdominal groans). Other features may include anorexia, nausea, vomiting, thirst, polyuria, fatigue and calcium deposits in the conjunctiva.

Q7.7
A = True
B = True
C = True
D = True
E = True
Carcinoma of the bronchus may exhibit certain nonmetastatic extra-pulmonary complications such as weight loss, anorexia, malaise, hyper-calcaemia, SIADH (syndrome of inappropriate ADH secretion), encephalopathy, motor neurone disease, peripheral neuropathy, myopathies, throm-bophlebitis migrans, disseminated intravascular coagulation, haemolytic anaemia, hypertrophic pulmonary osteoarthropathy, dermatomyositis, acanthosis nigricans and clubbing.

Q7.8
A = True
B = False
C; = False
D = True
E = True
The most common causes of acute pericarditis in the United Kingdom are myocardial infarction and Coxsackie virus infection. Dresler's syndrome is the development of a fever with pericarditis and pleural inflammation fol-lowing a myocardial infarction. Other causes of acute pericarditis include uraemia, connective tissue diseases, trauma, rheumatic fever, tuberculosis and malignancy. Myxoedema may rarely present with a pericardial effusion but not with acute pericarditis.

Q7.9
A = False
B = True
C = True
D = True
E = False
Clubbing is present when the normal angle between the base of the nail and the nail fold is lost. The base of the nail is fluctuant due to increased vascularity and the nail becomes more curved in all directions with expan-sion of the end of the finger. Causes of clubbing include carcinoma of the bronchus, bronchiectasis, lung abscess, empyema, pulmonary fibrosis, pleural and mediastinal tumours. Non-respiratory causes include congeni-tal clubbing, cyanotic congenital heart disease, bacterial endocarditis, inflammatory bowel disease and cirrhosis. Clubbing is not seen in chronic

bronchitis; its presence should prompt you to suspect another cause (e.g. bronchial carcinoma).

Q7.10
A = True
B = True
C = True
D = True
E = False
Ulcerative colitis may be complicated by carcinoma of the colon, particularly if the disease has been longstanding. Other conditions that may be associated with it include erythema nodosum, pyoderma gangrenosum, arthritis, liver disease (including sclerosing cholangitis), iritis and stomatitis. Stricture formation is characteristic of Crohn's disease, not ulcerative colitis.

Q7.11
A = True
B = False
C = False
D = True
E = False
Thyrotoxicosis classically presents with increased appetite, weight loss, a preference for cold weather, tachycardia or atrial fibrillation, tremor, anxiety and a proximal myopathy. A goitre may be present, as may exophthalmos, lid lag and lid retraction. Pretibial myxoedema is an infiltration of mucopolysaccharides into the subcutaneous tissues of the shin and occurs only in the presence of thyroid eye disease. It appears as a pink/purplish raised well demarcated area. Menorrhagia and sensitivity to the cold are characteristic of hypothyroidism.

Q7.12
A = False
B = True
C = True
D = True
E = False
The reticulocyte count in iron deficiency anaemia will only rise when iron is administered and can be used to monitor therapy. In sickle cell trait less than 40%–50% of the red cells contain haemoglobin S. Patients are asymptomatic unless subjected to severe hypoxia (e.g. at high altitudes) or if complications arise during anaesthesia. Pernicious anaemia is associated with malabsorption of vitamin B12 and results in a macrocytic anaemia.

Hereditary spherocytosis is characterised by a defect in the cell membrane protein spectrin which results in the cell losing membrane as it passes through the spleen. As the surface-to-volume ratio of the red blood cells is reduced, the cells become spherocytes and their lifespan is shortened. Polycythaemia rubra vera is caused by a chronic increase in the production of red cells by the bone marrow. This can result in increased blood viscosity and a higher risk of perioperative stroke and myocardial infarction, particularly if untreated; however, the red cell fragility is normal and there is no increased risk of haemolysis.

Q7.13
A = False
B = True
C = False
D = True
E = True

Cystic fibrosis is an autosomal-recessive disease resulting in dysfunction of all exocrine glands, which produce excessively thick and viscid secretions. The carrier frequency in Caucasians is 1 in 20–25, with a disease incidence of 1 in 2000 live births. The heterozygous state is not associated with any increase in respiratory disease. It is a multisystem disease affecting the respiratory, pancreatic and hepatobiliary systems, and cirrhosis and diabetes may occur. Early presentation in infancy with recurrent chest infections or meconium ileus and failure to thrive is common. A sweat test reveals abnormally high levels of sodium and chloride. Longterm management aims at ensuring effective lung drainage, with postural physiotherapy and control of bacterial infection. Life expectancy has been improved and survival into adulthood is common. Development of bronchiectasis, chronic bronchitis and recurrent pneumonia is a feature and in later stages lung or heart–lung transplantation may be required.

Q7.14
A = False
B = True
C = True
D = True
E = False

The anaemia of chronic renal disease is characteristically normocytic and normochromic. A haemoglobin concentration of 7–8 g dl^{-1} is usual in this condition if untreated. It is related to erythropoietin deficiency and a shortened erythrocyte life span. Hypertension usually occurs, mainly due to sodium retention and continuing renin secretion. The bleeding abnormality is characterised by a normal PT and aPTT and a qualitative platelet defect, although usually with a normal platelet count. This results in poor platelet attachment to the subendothelium and decreased platelet aggregation.

The skin changes result from a combination of anaemia and build-up of carotene-like pigments in the skin. Chronic itching may occur, which may be due to urea and/or calcium deposits in the skin.

Renal osteodystrophy is the result of the damaged kidneys being unable to produce 1,25-dihydrocholecalciferol, which is essential for the normal mineralisation of bone and the absorption of calcium from the gut. This results in osteomalacia, and the low serum calcium may cause secondary and ultimately tertiary hyperparathyroidism. The final bone abnormality in chronic renal failure is osteosclerosis, which may be a direct result of the raised parathyroid hormone levels. Osteoporosis does not characteristically occur.

Q7.15
A = True
B = True
C = False
D = True
E = False

Plummer–Vinson syndrome (or Paterson–Kelly syndrome) is comprised of an upper oesophageal web associated with iron deficiency anaemia. Symptoms include pain and difficulty on swallowing, which resolve with treatment of the iron deficiency. Achalasia of the cardia and pharyngeal pouch may also present with dysphagia, but their incidence is not increased in Plummer–Vinson syndrome.

Q7.16
A = False
B = False
C = True
D = True
E = True

Type 1 diabetes occurs predominantly in younger people and presents with weight loss, polyuria, polydipsia, infection, especially of the skin or urinary tract, and hyperglycaemic coma or precoma. Necrobiosis lipoidica is rare but pathognomonic of diabetes, and may preceed its presentation. It occurs as violet rings over the shins with yellow masses at the edges and scarring and atrophy at the centre.

Q7.17
A = False
B = True
C = True
D = False
E = False

Carcinoid is a rare disorder resulting from malignant carcinoid tumour, usually of the ileum, which has metastasised to the liver. The tumours predominantly secrete 5-hydroxytryptamine (serotonin), but may also produce other biologically active agents such as bradykinin, histamine or adrenocorticotrophic hormone (ACTH). Clinical effects include flushing of the skin, hypotension, hypertension, tachycardia, diarrhoea and bronchospasm. Prior to the development of metastasis the 5-hydroxytryptamine secreted into the portal circulation is metabolised rapidly by the liver, so that at this stage the tumour is asymptomatic. Carcinoid tumours of the bronchus and appendix also occur but rarely metastasise. Raised urinary VMA and paroxysmal hypertension are characteristic of phaeochromocytoma, not of carcinoid.

Q7.18
A = True
B = True
C = False
D = False
E = False

Right bundle branch block is characterised by an RSR pattern in V1 and a slurred S in V6. Left bundle branch block is indicated by a small Q wave in V1 and M pattern in V6. The QT interval is prolonged in hypocalcaemia and shortened in hypercalcaemia. The P wave may be bifid in left atrial hypertrophy (e.g. mitral stenosis) and peaked in right atrial hypertrophy (e.g. in pulmonary hypertension). Hyperkalaemia is associated with peaked T waves and hypokalaemia is associated with a U wave following the T wave.

Q7.19
A =True
B = False
C = False
D = True
E = True

Addison's disease is the result of destruction of the entire adrenal cortex, most commonly by autoimmune disease. Other causes include tuberculosis, malignancy and haemorrhage. It may present with grey/brown pigmentation of the buccal mucosa, hands, flexor creases and recent scars. There may also be weakness, weight loss, anorexia and fatigue. Serum sodium, cortisol and glucose may be low, whereas serum potassium, ACTH, urea and calcium may be high. Hypertension and a proximal myopathy are features of Cushing's syndrome, not Addison's disease.

Q7.20
A = False
B = False
C = True
D = True
E = True

Fallot's tetralogy consists of a ventricular septal defect, right ventricular outflow tract obstruction, an overriding aorta and right ventricular hypertrophy. It occurs in 15% of infants with congenital cardiac disease. It may be diagnosed antenatally or after birth, but usually presents after the neonatal period with cyanosis or the presence of cyanotic spells. Older children characteristically squat during a cyanotic spell, in order to increase the systemic vascular resistance by decreasing arterial blood flow to the legs. This results in an increase in the left-to-right shunt across the VSD and so increases pulmonary blood flow. Femoral pulses are normal. Diminished femoral pulses are associated with coarctation of the aorta.

Q7.21
A= True
B = False
C = False
D = False
E = True

Rheumatoid arthritis is a multisystem disease affecting three times more women than men. The hands and wrists are commonly affected and carpal tunnel syndrome occurs frequently. Pulmonary changes include pleural effusions, rheumatoid nodules within the lung parenchyma and pleural tissues. Respiratory symptoms tend to occur late in the disease and are restrictive rather than obstructive in nature. Alantoaxial subluxation is defined as a separation of greater than 3 mm between the body of the atlas and the odontoid peg. The odontoid process may compress the vertebral arteries and the medulla if it encroaches on the foramen magnum. Subaxial subluxation may also occur, causing cord compression. Tracheal intubation may be made difficult because of temperomandibular joint arthritis, which limits mouth opening, and also because of restricted neck mobility.

Q7.22
A = True
B = False
C = False
D = True
E = False

Anaemia is common in end-stage renal failure. It is due to a combination of factors including reduced red cell production and survival, increased losses due to peptic ulceration, poor nutrition with chronic deficiency in iron, vitamin B6, B12 and folate.

Morphine metabolites accumulate in renal failure. One of the most pharmacologically active is morphine–6–glucuronide, and high cerebral levels result in an increased risk of respiratory depression. Patients with chronic renal failure have decreased protein levels and protein binding, therefore any protein-bound drugs will have increased free component and activity.

Hypocalcaemia may be present but, due to the metabolic acidosis, the level of ionised calcium is usually within normal levels and symptoms are uncommon. The low calcium levels stimulate production of parathyroid hormones and this mobilises calcium and raises the level.

Epidurals are usually avoided due to the risk of bleeding. The coagulopathy associated with chronic renal failure is mainly a result of adequate numbers of poorly functioning platelets so that there is prolongation of the skin bleeding time with a normal platelet count, PT and PTT.

Q7.23
A = False
B = False
C = True
D = True
E = False

A normal body mass index, BMI, is 20–25 (the body mass index is the weight in kilograms divided by the height in metres squared). Obesity occurs with a BMI of 25–30, and morbid obesity is defined as a BMI > 35. An alternative definition of morbid obesity is a weight greater than 50% above the average for a given height.

These patients are automatically designated as ASA IV, as there is increasing morbidity associated with morbid obesity. Severely obese patients have an increased incidence of hypertension, ischaemic heart disease, asthma, oesophageal reflux and decreased respiratory reserve (due to a diminished functional residual capacity (FRC), which may result in hypoxaemia due to increased airway closure and the development of intrapulmonary shunting). Many physiological changes occur with increasing weight. In the gastrointestinal system oesophageal reflux is common and hiatus hernia frequent. Increased intragastric volume and raised intra-abdominal pressure also occur, so the risk of perioperative aspiration is increased.

Glucose intolerance, abnormal carbohydrate metabolism and an increased incidence of diabetes all occur in this group. Anaphylaxis and obesity are not associated conditions.

Q7.24
A = False
B = True
C = True
D = True
E = False

Myasthenia gravis is an autoimmune disease in which the presence of autoantibodies to the acetylcholine receptor at the neuromuscular junction results in a decreased number of active receptor sites. This is characterised by muscle weakness and fatiguability with repetitive muscle activity. It is often noticed most in the face where there is diplopia and ptosis. 10% of cases of myasthenia gravis have an associated thymoma. Treatment includes the long-acting anticholinesterase pyridostigmine. Patients with myasthenia gravis are very sensitive to non-depolarising muscle relaxants and their response may be variable. Short-acting relaxants, which can be carefully titrated against neuromuscular function, should be used. As atracurium and cisatracurium are metabolised by Hoffman degradation, they are the relaxants of choice, although the dose should be decreased to 10%–20% of normal. Depolarising muscle relaxants such as suxamethonium do not cause increased fasciculations, but their action may be unpredictable in duration. Hypokalaemia, aminoglycosides, ciprofloxacin, magnesium and quinine all exacerbate the weakness associated with this condition. Eaton Lambert syndrome is a rare, myasthenia-like condition occurring in oat cell carcinoma of the bronchus. There is defective release of acetylcholine at the neuromuscular junction resulting in muscle weakness, which tends to improve on repeated activity, i.e. it is nonfatiguable. Anaesthetic management in this syndrome is similar to that of myasthenia gravis.

Q7.25
A = True
B = True
C = False
D = False
E = False

Prions are infective agents which consist of protease-resistant proteins without detectable DNA or RNA. They seem to be conformational variants of naturally occurring proteins and replicate by triggering the distortion of the normal protein into the abnormal shape of the prion via a protein–protein interaction. This is a purely physical reaction and can occur in cell-free preparations without any sort of metabolism

The prion that causes scrapie in sheep is thought to have crossed the species barrier to produce bovine spongiform encephalopathy. This is considered to be the cause of vCJD in humans. Scrapie occurs in sheep, not in cattle, and is known not to affect humans eating sheep products.

This disease appears to predominantly, but not exclusively, affect the young. However, the average incubation period may be as long as 20–30 years. The prions which cause the infection are concentrated in brain, spinal cord and nervous tissue of the affected cattle, not in blood, milk or bone. In humans, single-use equipment has been recommended for surgery in certain areas such as brain biopsy, spinal cord surgery and tonsillectomy, as the prions have been found concentrated there. This is in order to prevent the possibility of cross-contamination in these selected cases. This is however under review following adverse incidents with the use of single-use adeno-tonsillectomy equipment. Potential risk of transmission from blood products is under investigation.

Q7.26
A = True
B = True
C = False
D = True
E = True

Seroconversion following a Hepatitis B-contaminated needle-stick injury is 5%–30%, much higher that the risk with HIV-contaminated injuries. Frequently a patient will be unaware of their positive HIV status and can be asymptomatic. Common symptoms which may develop slowly include tiredness, anorexia, respiratory infection, nausea, vomiting, abdominal discomfort, rash, joint pains and fever. Transmission of hepatitis C has frequently occurred via administration of blood products, but a well documented Australian case showed that inter-patient infection could occur via the breathing systems if adequate fresh gas filtration was not used. Hepatitis C cirrhosis is now the most common indication for liver transplantation internationally.

Q7.27

A = True
B = False
C = True
D = True
E = True

Cancer patients are treated with various regimens of chemotherapy, surgery and/or radiotherapy. Complications must be considered before anaesthesia is undertaken. Bleomycin tends to accumulate in the lung, and the use of oxygen therapy increases the risk of development of pulmonary fibrosis. Cardiac complications are common with some chemotherapeutic agents but not with methotrexate. Doxorubicin use may cause a dose-related cardio-myopathy, non-specific T-wave changes and atrial and ventricular ectopics. Thoracic irradiation is associated with development of pneumonitis, which usually resolves spontaneously; however, radiation fibrosis may develop later. Initial chemotherapeutic treatment of some conditions such as ALL can be associated with an acute tumour lysis syndrome, which causes hyperkalaemia, hyperuricaemia, hyperphosphataemia (due to the large abnormal cellular content load when lysed) and the development of acute renal failure. Treatment of acute tumour lysis includes intravenous fluids, alkalisation of the urine with allopurinol.

Q7.28

A = False
B = False
C = True
D = False
E = False

Diabetic retinopathy is one of the most common causes of blindness. It is due to microangiopathy in the retina and develops more rapidly if blood sugar control is poor. Similar effects of microangiopathy of the vasa nervorum can cause both sympathetic and parasympathetic dysfunction. Retrolental fibroplasia is a condition of premature neonates. The aetiology is multifactorial but risk factors include hyperoxia.

Episodes of orthostatic hypotension are related to a lack of sympathetic vasoconstriction mechanisms. These mechanisms also lead to painless myocardial ischaemic episodes, which can be difficult to identify. Type 1, juvenile-onset diabetes usually requires insulin management, whereas with late-onset type 2 diabetes, insulin is frequently not required. While the more common presentation of coma is of a ketoacidotic type, a hyper-osmolar, non-ketotic coma does occur, particularly in the older patient with mild diabetes.

Q7.29
A = True
B = True
C = False
D = False
E = False

Signs of advanced liver disease include tiredness, ascites, encephalopathy, peripheral oedema, hyperdynamic circulation, glucose intolerance, jaundice, abdominal pain, delayed gastric emptying, bleeding varices (gastric or oesophageal), low albumin levels and raised prothrombin time. Mortality is extremely high in this condition. If transplantation is achieved, then the survival can be above 70% at one year.

Paracetamol overdose remains the most common cause of acute liver failure. Early mortality is usually from prolonged intracranial pressure due to cerebral oedema. Later death will result from liver failure, hepatorenal syndrome and multisystem failure.

Transplantation is undertaken in patients with alcoholic cirrhosis, but usually after they have benefited from a period of abstinence from alcohol.

Q7.30
A = False
B = True
C = True
D = True
E = False

Magnesium is predominantly an intracellular ion. 55% of serum magnesium is in the ionised form, which is clinically active. Common causes of hypomagnesaemia include diuretic use, alcohol withdrawal and reduced absorption from the gut due to laxative abuse, fistulae or malabsorption. Hypermagnesaemia may be iatrogenic, with administration of the drug for cardiac disease or pre-eclampsia, via parentral nutrition or enemas. Hypomagnesaemia may result in arrhythmias, heart failure, vasospasm (e.g. of the coronary arteries), nausea, anorexia, abdominal pain, tetany, seizures, muscle spasms, weakness and psychosis. Hypermagnesaemia results in decreased deep tendon reflexes, bradycardia, hypotension, heart block, respiratory insufficiency and, if very high levels are present, cardiac arrest may occur.

It is hypomagnesaemia which increases digitalis toxicity.

Q7.31
A = True
B = True
C = True
D = True
E = True

Thromboembolic disease is common after major surgery, and pulmonary embolism resulting in death most commonly occurs as a result of deep vein thrombosis. Factors causing these changes include sluggish blood flow, injury to the blood vessels and the presence of any hypercoaguability state such as deficiencies in antithrombin III, protein C or protein S. Risk factors for thromboembolic disease include advancing age, surgery or immobility from any cause, malignancy, pregnancy, oral contraceptive use, sickle cell disease and obesity. Venous thrombosis is particularly common following trauma or hip surgery, urological surgery, gynaecology or neurosurgery.

Factor V Leiden is the most common hereditary blood coagulation disorder. It is present in 3%–8% of Caucasians and is associated with an increased risk of secondary and spontaneous venous thromboembolism, especially in those taking the oral contraceptive pill.

Q7.32
A = True
B = True
C = False
D = False
E = False

Multiple myeloma results from a proliferation of plasma cells. There is an increase in serum immunoglobulins and the specific type is identified by electrophoresis of either urine or blood. Renal damage may occur. Other features include bone marrow failure, hypercalcaemia, pathological fractures and bone pain.

Postsplenectomy, Howell–Jolly bodies and target cells are seen in the blood film, and Heinz bodies may also be identified if special staining techniques are used. The Chief Medical Officer has advised that all patients who have had a splenectomy should carry cards identifying this situation.

Acute lymphocytic leukaemia tends to occur predominantly but not exclusively in the young. Chronic myeloid leukaemia affects young and middle-aged patients and is associated with the Philadelphia chromosome which, when present, is associated with a longer survival period. Hodgkin's is a cancer of the lymphatic tissues and the blood film may be normal.

Alternatively a normocytic anaemia may occur, the white count may be low, normal or high, eosinophilia or monocytosis may occur. Abnormalities in platelets are not characteristic of Hodgkin's disease.

8. Surgery

Q8.1. In a 60-year-old male suffering from acute pancreatitis the following factors may be used to assess the severity of the disease:

A. age
B. serum calcium
C. agonising abdominal pain
D. bruising in the loins (Grey Turner's sign)
E. arterial PaO_2

Q8.2. Following a road traffic accident in which a passenger was thrown from the car, the following may lead you to suspect lung contusion:

A. haemopneumothorax
B. the history
C. flail segment
D. cardiac arrhythmias
E. several rib fractures but no wheeze or crepitations on auscultation of the chest on arrival in casualty

Q8.3. You are called to see a 66-year-old patient in recovery who has undergone a laparotomy to oversew a bleeding duodenal ulcer. On examination she is pale and sweaty, the blood pressure is 110/60, the pulse is 126 beats/min, temperature 37.8°C and the central venous pressure 2 cm H_2O. This is consistent with:

A. overtransfusion
B. sepsis
C. hypovolaemia
D. congestive cardiac failure
E. continued bleeding from the ulcer

Q8.4. A tourniquet applied to the leg to achieve a bloodless field for surgery:

A. should not be inflated for more than one hour
B. is contraindicated in patients with HbAS
C. should be inflated to 100 mm Hg above the systolic blood pressure to be effective
D. should not be used in conjunction with regional anaesthetic techniques
E. should have a cuff whose width is two-thirds the length of the thigh

Q8.5. Duodenal ulceration is:

A. more common in males than in females
B. associated with risk of malignant change if longstanding
C. increased in cigarette smokers
D. possibly infective in origin
E. severe in Zollinger–Ellison syndrome

Q8.6. Haematuria may be associated with:

A. benign prostatic hypertrophy
B. carcinoma of the prostate
C. carcinoma of the bladder
D. glomerulonephritis
E. infective endocarditis

Q8.7 A ruptured oesophagus may present with:

A. surgical emphysema
B. tenderness in the suprasternal notch
C. gas under the diaphragm on chest x-ray
D. a pneumothorax with the presence of a fluid level on the chest x-ray
E. sudden severe chest pain

Q8.8 Volkmann's ischaemic contracture may occur following:

A. application of a tight plaster cast
B. dislocation of the elbow
C. mastectomy and axillary clearance
D. axillary vein thrombosis
E. carpal tunnel syndrome

Q8.9 In a 55-year-old woman presenting with a single breast lump:

A. mammography should be carried out
B. it is likely to be benign at this age; thus it may initially be kept under review
C. *peau d'orange* suggests carcinoma
D. palpable axillary lymph nodes indicates metastatic involvement
E. needle aspiration is contraindicated

Q8.10 Acute renal failure may be precipitated following major surgery by:

A. prolonged hypotension
B. obstructive jaundice
C. septicaemia
D. pre-existing renal disease
E. haemolysis

Q8.11 An aortic aneurysm may present with:

A. dysphagia
B. aortic incompetence
C. sciatica
D. back pain
E. bruising around the umbilicus (Cullen's sign)

Q8.12 In a patient with atrial fibrillation a blood clot may travel from the left atrium to occlude one of the femoral arteries, resulting in:

A. pain
B. a white leg
C. absent peripheral pulses
D. paraesthesia
E. muscular weakness

Q8.13 Surgical emphysema may be associated with the following:

A. a bronchial tear
B. massive air embolism
C. flail chest
D. the bends
E. chest drain insertion

Q8.14 Acute appendicitis:

A. is more common in children under 10 years of age
B. may present with tenderness in the right iliac fossa on palpation of the left iliac fossa
C. the signs may be identical to those of a sickle cell crisis
D. the signs may be identical to those of an inflamed Meckel's diverticulum
E. pain on passive extension of the leg may be present (psoas sign)

Q8.15 In the first 24 hours following major surgery:

A. sodium excretion is reduced
B. antidiuretic hormone levels increase
C. hypoglycaemia is common
D. urinary excretion of nitrogen increases
E. the plasma level of cortisol is decreased

Q8.16 Abdominal ultrasound is useful in confirming the diagnosis of:

A. portal hypertension
B. carcinoma of the colon
C. ascites
D. gall stones
E. hydatidiform mole

Q8.17 The following features would support the dignosis of acute bowel obstruction in a 50-year-old female admitted with abdominal pain:

A. absent bowel sounds
B. tinkling bowel sounds
C. guarding and rebound tenderness
D. visible peristalsis
E. gas under the diaphragm on the chest x-ray

Q8.18 Fractures associated with avascular necrosis include:

A. fracture of the head of the radius
B. scaphoid fracture
C. fracture of the neck of the femur
D. supracondylar fracture of the humerus
E. fractured talus

Q8.19 Complications associated with open splenectomy include:

A. pancreatitis
B. right lower lobe collapse
C. major haemorrhage
D. deep venous thrombosis
E. pneumococcal infection

Q8.20 The following may complicate hysteroscopy and endometrial resection:

A. postoperative menorrhagia
B. uterine perforation
C. transurethral resection (TUR) syndrome
D. air embolism
E. severe pain

Q8.21. When consent for treatment is requested:

A. there must always be a signed consent form
B. the next of kin may consent for an 'incompetent adult' to undergo a procedure
C. a child under 16 years of age may consent to treatment against parental wishes
D. advance refusal of treatment is legally binding
E. consent must be sought within two weeks of the procedure

Q8.22. When performing a tracheostomy:

A. a tracheal flap is less likely than a slit to result in tracheal stenosis
B. percutaneous methods are indicated in patients with coagulopathy
C. early complications may include pneumothorax
D. tract formation occurs within three days
E. tracheal stenosis always requires surgical correction

Q8.23 A 75-year-old woman presents with a fractured neck of the femur for surgical repair. She is taking warfarin for longstanding atrial fibrillation. Her preoperative INR is 5, and Hb is 9 g dl⁻¹. Acceptable management includes:

A. packed cell transfusion to Hb 12 g dl⁻¹ and vitamin K injection
B. stopping warfarin, giving iron supplements and operating when INR ≤ 2
C. stop warfarin, correct coagulopathy with haematological advice and operate on the next available list
D. operate immediately with fresh frozen plasma being infused
E. treat conservatively

Q8.24 Concerning laparoscopic techniques:

A. pneumoperitoneum is achieved using carbon monoxide
B. there is a risk of explosion using diathermy if nitrous oxide is the insufflating gas
C. disposable operating ports are latex-free
D. recommended safe maximum limits for insufflation are 10 litres total gas volume and 6 kPa intra-abdominal pressure
E. postoperative morbidity is reduced when compared with 'open' techniques

Q8.25 The following statements are true of tracheo-oesophageal fistula:

A. it is more common in preterm infants
B. it usually presents at 6 to 8 weeks postnatally
C. the surgical priority is to close the fistula
D. most patients can be extubated immediately postoperatively
E. mortality is higher in low-birthweight babies

Q8.26 Exomphalos:

A. is a defect of the abdominal wall lateral to the umbilicus
B. is a herniation into the umbilical cord
C. is commonly associated with thoracic and cardiac abnormalities
D. is less common that gastroschisis
E. mortality due to this condition is lower than mortality from gastroschisis

Q8.27 The following statements are true of placenta praevia:

A. it is more likely to occur with a history of previous caesarian sections
B. in grade II the placenta covers most of the cervical os
C. it is associated with an increased risk of postpartum haemorrhage
D. malpresentation of the foetus is more common
E. the usual mode of delivery is vaginal

Q8.28 Concerning thyroid lumps:

A. solitary thyroid lumps are usually malignant
B. retrosternal goitres invariably require sternotomy to facilitate operative excision
C. Graves' disease has a familial incidence
D. radioactive iodine is the management of choice in thyrotoxic patients under 50 years of age
E. carbimazole will cause a goitre to shrink and become less vascular

Q8.29 Concerning perioperative nerve injuries:

A. clawing of the hand and loss of sensation on the medial border of the hand may result from compression injuries at the elbow
B. prolonged lithotomy positioning may result in foot drop
C. median nerve damage results in wrist drop
D. paraesthesia in the lateral 3½ fingers results from excessive tourniquet pressure on the spiral groove of the humerus
E. intramuscular injections in the buttock may result in loss of sensation below the knee

Q8.30 In patients with a fractured neck of femur:

A. Spinal anaesthesia is the method of choice
B. there is a decreased mortality if managed with epidural anaesthesia
C. tolerance of anaesthesia with isoflurane, nitrous oxide and oxygen is poor
D. there is an increased risk of deep venous thrombosis
E. hypotensive anaesthesia is necessary

Answers to Section 8

Q8.1
A = True
B = True
C = False
D = False
E = True

A number of clinical and laboratory criteria have been defined which have prognostic significance in acute pancreatitis. The presence of three or more of these criteria indicates severe disease:

- age > 55
- systolic blood pressure < 90 mm Hg
- white blood count > 15×10^9 litre^{-1}
- temperature > 39°C
- blood glucose (no diabetic history) > 10 mmol litre^{-1}
- plasma urea > 15 mmol litre^{-1}
- PaO_2 < 8kPa
- serum calcium < 2 mmol litre^{-1}
- serum albumin < 32g litre^{-1}
- haematocrit reduced by over 10%
- abnormal liver function tests

Severe abdominal pain, typically radiating through to the back, and Grey Turner's sign do occur but are not reliable indicators of disease severity.

Q8.2
A = True
B = True
C = True
D = False
E = True

Pulmonary contusion is a common and potentially lethal chest injury. Respiratory failure may develop over the subsequent 2–3 days, and in severe cases it may become impossible to ventilate the lungs. Lung contusion is associated with severe chest injury and, although there may be no ventilatory compromise on arrival in casualty, it should always be suspected in the presence of evidence of severe chest trauma. In a child, lung contusion may occur without fracture of the flexible overlying ribs; here the history is important, and being thrown from a car indicates a potentially severe injury. Cardiac arrhythmias are suggestive of cardiac contusion.

Q8.3
A = False
B = True
C = True
D = False
E = True

Overtransfusion is associated with hypertension, bradycardia and a high central venous pressure. Conversely, congestive cardiac failure is associated with a low blood pressure, tachycardia and a high central venous pressure.

Q8.4
A = False
B = False
C = True
D = False
E = False

A tourniquet applied to the leg may be inflated for up to two hours, although the risk of complications increases with increasing duration. Care should be taken applying it to avoid nerve damage. Tourniquets are probably best avoided in sickle cell disease, but are acceptable in sickle cell trait, with careful exsanguination prior to tourniquet application. The width of the cuff is not related to the length of the thigh, but it is usual to choose the largest appropriate cuff.

Q8.5
A = True
B = False
C = True
D = True
E = True

The male-to-female ratio of duodenal ulceration is 10:1. Duodenal ulcers differ from gastric ulcers in that there is no risk of malignant change however longstanding they are. The Gram-negative bacillus *Helicobacter pylori* is implicated in the aeitiology of duodenal ulceration; about 70% of patients with peptic ulcers have evidence of infection which can be detected with the [13]Carbon-urea breath test. Eradication of *H. pylori* infection with tetracycline, metronidazole, bismuth subcinate and omeprazole may effect a 98% cure rate of peptic ulcers. The Zollinger–Ellison syndrome is due to a gastrin-secreting tumour leading to hypersecretion of gastric acid. This results in severe ulceration which may involve the stomach, duodenum, and jejunum.

Q8.6
A = True
B = True
C = True
D = True
E = True
Haematuria should always be fully investigated. Other causes include coagulopathies, renal tract malignancies, urinary tract stones, renal trauma and infarction. Malignant hypertension, polyarteritis nodosa, Henoch–Schönlein purpura, polycystic kidneys, haemorrhagic diseases and systemic lupus erythematosus are also causes of haematuria.

Q8.7
A = True
B = True
C = True
D = True
E = True
Tenderness in the suprasternal notch at the side of the oesophagus is an early sign of ruptured oesophagus, and the chest x-ray sign of pleural effusion associated with a pneumothorax is virtually pathognomonic. Gas beneath the diaphragm may occur if the abdominal oesophagus is perforated; the clinical features then resemble those of a perforated peptic ulcer. Pyrexia is common. The management of a ruptured oesophagus includes urgent surgical repair to minimise the degree of mediastinal contamination.

Q8.8
A = True
B = True
C = False
D = False
E = False
Volkmann's ischaemic contracture is caused by ischaemia of the flexor muscles of the forearm and hand due to obstruction of the brachial artery near the elbow or by the presence of tense oedema of the soft tissues of the forearm within the constraints of a fascial compartment. This results in a flexion deformity of the wrist and fingers.

Q8.9
A = True
B = False
C = True
D = False
E = False

Common causes of breast lump include benign mammary dysplasia, benign neoplasms, malignant neoplasms and fat necrosis. A breast lump in a post-menopausal woman has a high probability of being malignant in origin. Mammography is useful and may show an opacity containing microcalcifications; it may also reveal other lesions elsewhere in the breast. Ultrasonography is also used for breast imaging and screening. Diagnosis may be confirmed with needle aspiration or true-cut biopsy in the out-patient department. Open excision biopsy may be necessary. Palpable lymph nodes may be reactive and do not necessarily imply tumour involvement.

Q8.10
A = True
B = True
C = True
D = True
E = True

Prolonged hypotension during surgery results in splanchnic vasoconstriction and impaired renal perfusion. Patients with obstructive jaundice are at risk of developing hepatorenal syndrome; the cause is uncertain but the renal failure may be prevented by maintaining adequate hydration and continuing diuresis ($1 \, ml \, min^{-1}$). Mannitol may have a role in the management of these patients. Haemolysis (e.g. that associated with a transfusion reaction) releases free haemoglobin into the circulation, which is then filtered by the kidney and may block renal tubules, resulting in renal failure.

Q8.11
A = True
B = True
C = True
D = True
E = False

A thoracic aortic aneurysm may cause dysphagia by compressing the oesophagus; hoarseness may also result from pressure on the recurrent laryngeal nerve. An aneurysm may undergo dissection; in the case of a thoracic aneurysm the dissection may extend back to the aortic valve, resulting in aortic incompetence. An abdominal aortic aneurysm may cause sciatica by compressing the sciatic nerve. Periumbilical bruising (Cullen's sign) occurs with acute pancreatitis.

Q8.12
A = True
B = True
C = True
D = True
E = True

Peripheral arterial embolism is characteristically associated with the embolisation of mural thrombus in patients with atrial fibrillation or cardiac failure. 50% of patients suffering from an arterial embolus have atrial fibrillation and 30% have a proven recent myocardial infarction. Cardioversion may also precipitate embolisation, therefore it is current practice to anticoagulate patients before undergoing cardioversion. The characteristic symptoms caused by the embolus (the five Ps) are pain, pallor, pulselessness, paraesthesia and paralysis.

Q8.13
A = True
B = False
C = True
D = False
E = True

Surgical emphysema occurs as a result of air in the tissue planes. This may be secondary to a severe chest injury, lung injury, or a flail segment. It may also be associated with formation of tracheostomy or insertion of a chest drain. The air enters the tissues when there is injury to the airway or lung and may spread widely over the chest, abdomen, neck and face. It subsides spontaneously over several days and usually requires no specific treatment.

Q8.14
A = False
B = True
C = True
D = True
E = True

Acute appendicitis is most common in the second and third decades. Typically it presents with periumbilical pain which later becomes localised to the right iliac fossa. Rovsig's sign (pressure in the left iliac fossa causing right-sided pain) may be present, as may the psoas sign. It is very important to differentiate between surgical causes of abdominal pain and an acute sickle cell crisis in susceptible patients by examining blood films. The abdominal pain in a sickle cell crisis is due to acute vascular occlusion within intra-abdominal organs by the distorted sickle shaped red blood cells. This may result in papillary necrosis of the kidney, peptic ulceration and sequestration crises. Sickle cell patients are also prone to gallstone formation.

Q8.15
A = True
B = True
C = False
D = True
E = False

There is a 'stress response' in the first 24 hours following major surgery; the plasma levels of ADH, cortisol, growth hormone, glucagon, prolactin and the catacholamines rise. Cortisol may rise to five times normal levels and remain elevated for several days; this causes salt and water retention and also inhibits the action of insulin. The patient enters a catabolic phase in which protein is broken down to release nitrogen, which is then excreted by the kidneys, resulting in a negative nitrogen balance.

Q8.16
A = True
B = False
C = True
D = True
E = True

The probe of an ultrasound machine houses the transducer; this is a piezo-electric crystal which, when electronically activated, produces pulses of very high frequency sound called ultrasound. Ultrasound travels in straight lines until it reaches an interface, i.e. a boundary between two tissues with different acoustic velocities. Here part of the wave is reflected from the interface and the remainder is propagated through the second tissue. In this way fluid appears dark, while fat and other tissues appear white and varying shades of grey. Thus, increasing the diameter of the portal vein in portal hypertension can be indicated by the increased distance between the two 'white' walls and the 'dark' contents of the vessel. Ascites appears black, gall stones appear white and are highly echogenic, and a hydatidiform mole has a classic 'snowstorm' appearance. However, at gas-soft tissue interfaces almost all the beam is reflected so that scanning through bowel is impossible.

Q8.17

A = False
B = True
C = False
D = True
E = False

The clinical features of intestinal obstruction include colicky abdominal pain and constipation. Vomiting may occur, but may be absent in distal small bowel or colonic obstruction. On examination abdominal distension is usually present, visible peristalsis may occur, and the bowel sounds become high-pitched and tinkling. Absent bowel sounds occur in ileus, guarding and rebound tenderness occur in peritonitis, and gas under the diaphragm implies a perforated viscus.

Q8.18

A = False
B = True
C = True
D = True
E = True

Avascular necrosis occurs when the blood supply to a bone or part of a bone is interrupted. The avascular fragment dies and gradually collapses over a period of years, eventually leading to osteoarthritis. Avascular necrosis occurs most frequently at the head of the femur after fracture of the femoral neck, the proximal half of the scaphoid bone, and the body of the talus.

Q8.19

A = True
B = False
C = True
D = True
E = True

Open splenectomy may result in major haemorrhage. Although bleeding from the pedicle should not occur, oozing from multiple adhesions is common. Also splenectomy may have been carried out for a bleeding disorder such as idiopathic thrombocytopaenia which will not be immediately corrected. Left lower lobe collapse is a local complication of splenectomy. As the spleen is a lymphoid organ, its loss reduces immunity and impairs the response to bacteraemia, especially in children. Prophylactic antibiotics and antipneumococcal vaccine will be required longterm.

Q8.20
A = False
B = True
C = True
D = True
E = False

Hysteroscopy and endometrial resection is a useful technique in the management of menorrhagia. The uterus is relatively insensitive to cutting and therefore severe pain is uncommon. The uterine cavity is constantly irrigated and distended with fluid during the procedure. Glycine-containing solutions are rarely used because of the risk of neurological symptoms following the absorption of glycine into the blood stream. These symptoms include transient blindness, and may be due to the activation of central inhibitory pathways. Current irrigation solutions contain sorbitol and mannitol. If large volumes are absorbed the resulting symptoms of fluid overload, hypertension, hyponatraemia and neurological signs are the same as those found in transurethral resection of prostate syndrome (TUR syndrome). Air embolism may occur via myometrial venous channels, and uterine perforation is always a potential complication of intrauterine surgery.

Q8.21
A = False
B = False
C = True
D = True
E = False

For consent to be valid, it must be given voluntarily by an appropriately informed person who has the capacity to consent to the intervention in question. It may be implied (e.g. in the case of cooperation during physical examination) or expressed (obtained for any procedure which carries a material risk). Validity of consent does not depend on the form in which it is given. Written consent merely serves as evidence of consent. In England and Wales, a 'competent adult' is over 18 years of age and has the capacity to make decisions on his/her own behalf regarding treatment. No other person can consent to treatment on behalf of an adult, although it is wise to consult with next-of-kin before treating an adult without consent (e.g. in the case of a sedated ITU patient). A 'Gillick-competent' child may consent to treatment, but refusal to treatment may, in certain circumstances, be overridden by a person with parental responsibility or a court. An advance refusal of treatment which is valid, and applicable to subsequent circumstances in which the patient lacks capacity, is legally binding. When a patient gives valid consent to an intervention, in general that consent remains valid for an indefinite duration unless it is withdrawn by the patient. Consent should be resought if the patient's condition changes, new information concerning the procedure is available, there is an altered risk or if the proposed intervention changes.

Q8.22
A = False
B = False
C = True
D = False
E = False

The surgical provision of a tracheostomy involves making a slit or circular opening in the trachea at the level of the 2nd, 3rd or 4th tracheal rings. The previously-used technique of creating a tracheal flap has been implicated in causing tracheal stenosis. The advantages of percutaneous tracheostomy include the ability of ITU staff to perform the procedure on the unit, thus avoiding the need to transfer critically ill ITU patients to theatres for an open procedure. However, the immediate and early complication rate is high in unskilled hands. Contraindications to performing a percutaneous tracheostomy include difficult anatomy and the presence of a coagulopathy. In these situations, the open procedure is preferable. Early complications of the open procedure include haemorrhage, tube displacement, tube blockage, surgical emphysema and pneumothorax. The initial tube is usually left in situ for at least a week to allow tract formation. Tracheal stenosis is a late complication of both open and percutaneous procedures. It usually occurs level with the stoma or tube cuff. Surgical resection may be required if conservative management or dilatation of the stenotic area are not successful.

Q8.23
A = False
B = False
C = True
D = False
E = False

There is considerable morbidity and mortality associated with fractured hips in the elderly population. Conservative management carries high mortality associated with the prolonged bed rest involved. Early operative management within 24–48 hours is associated with improved outcome as mobilisation is facilitated. Mortality at one month is reported variously as 5%–32%.

This patient should have her warfarin stopped. Haematological advice should be sought for the partial correction of her coagulaopathy (INR ≤1.8) within 12–24 hours and this will require the transfusion of fresh frozen plasma and possibly cryoprecipitate. If left to correct passively, the INR may take more than 5 days to reduce from 5 to 1.8. Vitamin K is usually not recommended as re-warfarinisation postoperatively will be hampered. The use of heparin in the perioperative period may increase the risk of haemorrhage in these patients, and stopping warfarin has not in fact been shown to markedly increase the risk of venous or arterial thromboembolism from the atrial clot in the short term. Patients who are anticoagulated because of the presence of mechanical heart valves or a recent history of thromboembolism (within one month) may need perioperative heparin to cover the warfarin-free period.

The patient's anaemia should be investigated (haematinics, blood film) and is probably due to blood loss from the fracture, although dietary insufficiency and bone marrow abnormalities are common in the elderly and may be contributory. It is acceptable to have an Hb $\geq 9\,\mathrm{g\,dl^{-1}}$ preoperatively, but blood must be available for transfusion. Older patients with additional premorbid abnormalities will tolerate low postoperative haemoglobin less well than the young and fit. Perioperative blood loss during a dynamic hip screw is usually less than 400 ml.

Q8.24
A = False
B = True
C = True
D = False
E = True

Laparoscopic techniques were initially confined to gynaecological surgery but are now increasingly used in all surgical specialities. The advantages include a reduced incidence of postoperative morbidity and pain. Pneumoperitoneum is induced, usually with carbon dioxide. This is absorbed across the peritoneum and may result in hypercapnoea. The most commonly used disposable ports are latex-free, although some of the older reusable ports have latex seals.

Gas insufflation may cause haemodynamic and respiratory compromise and therefore the following are recommended safe maximum limits for insufflation:
- 4 litre min^{-1}
- 3–5 litre total gas volume
- 3 kPa maximal intraperitoneal pressure (30 cm H_2O).

Q8.25

A = True
B = False
C = True
D = False
E = True

Oesophageal atresia, with or without a fistula, occurs in about 1 in 3500 live births. The main danger of the condition is the risk of aspiration and contamination of the lungs. It may be diagnosed antenatally, and is to be suspected in cases of polyhydramnios and premature labour. The condition is usually noted at birth with the baby drooling saliva from the mouth, and difficulty in feeding. Diagnosis is confirmed by the inability to pass a catheter down the oesophagus and into the stomach. There will be a gas bubble in the stomach apparent on chest x-ray if a fistula exists. The commonest anomaly (86%) is a combination of blind-ending upper pouch and lower pouch fistula; this is invariably diagnosed at birth. If no gas bubble is seen on chest x-ray, then the most likely diagnosis is atresia without a fistula (10%). Rarer anomalies (1% each) are tracheo-oesophageal fistula without oesophageal atresia; oesophageal atresia with upper pouch tracheo-oesophageal fistula; oesophageal atresia with tracheo-oesophageal fistulae to upper and lower pouches. Once the diagnosis has been made, the lungs are protected by passage of a Repogle tube into the upper pouch. This is a double-lumen sump tube through which continuous suction may be applied. This keeps the secretions clear and reduces the likelihood of aspiration. Operative correction is at the earliest convenient opportunity. 30%–50% of these babies have associated anomalies, especially cardiac,

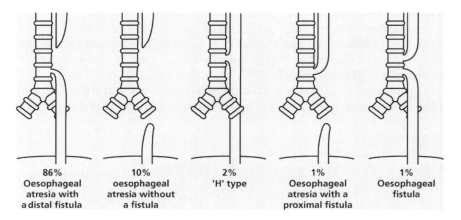

| 86% | 10% | 2% | 1% | 1% |
| Oesophageal atresia with a distal fistula | oesophageal atresia without a fistula | 'H' type | Oesophageal atresia with a proximal fistula | Oesophageal fistula |

Fig. 8.1: Tracheo–oesophageal fistula

respiratory, cleft lip and palate, and the VATER syndrome (a non-random association of defects: vertebral anomalies/VSD, anal atresia, tracheo-oesophageal fistula, oesophageal atresia, radial dysplasia/renal anomalies). About 50% of patients will require postoperative ventilation after repair of tracheo-oesophageal fistula.

Q8.26
A = False
B = True
C = True
D = False
E = True
Exomphalos (between 1 in 5000 and 1 in 10 000 live births) is a herniation into the umbilical cord. Gastroschisis (1 in 30 000 live births) is a defect in the abdominal wall lateral to the umbilicus, usually on the right side. Exomphalos is commonly associated with thoracic and cardiac abnormalities, whereas gastroschisis has no such associations. Mortality is rarely due to the exomphalos but is due to associated major cardiac or respiratory abnormalities. Mortality from gastroschisis remains fairly high.

Q8.27
A = True
B = False
C = True
D = True
E = False
Placenta praevia occurs when there is encroachment of the placenta upon the cervical os. Four grades are described:
I   low-lying placenta
II   placenta reaches the os
III placenta covers the os
IV   placenta is placed squarely over the os

Placenta praevia occurs in 0.25% of all pregnancies, but this is increased in those with a history of previous caesarian section. Complications include antepartum and postpartum haemorrhage, malpresentation and placenta accreta. Delivery of the foetus is usually by caesarian section.

Q8.28
A = False
B = False
C = True
D = False
E = False

10% of solitary thyroid lumps are malignant. 82% of retrosternal goitres can be excised via a standard incision. Graves' thyrotoxicosis is an autoimmune disease with an increased incidence in certain families and association with other autoimmune conditions such as myasthenia gravis, pernicious anaemia and Addison's disease. Patients with thyrotoxicosis under the age of 50 are usually treated medically in the first instance but are surgically managed thereafter. Radioactive iodine is usually offered to patients over the age of 50. Carbimazole blocks the production of thyroxine and may be used to render the thyrotoxic patient euthyroid preoperatively. It does, however, cause the thyroid gland to become larger and more vascular and must be stopped 10 days before the operation is planned.

Q8.29
A = True
B = True
C = False
D = False
E = True

The ulnar nerve (C7–T1) is a terminal branch of the medial cord of the brachial plexus supplying sensation and motor innervation to the hand. It is most commonly injured at the elbow, where it lies behind the medial epicondyle. The result is the loss of cutaneous sensation to the ulnar 1½ fingers and the ulnar side of hand. Paralysis of the small muscles of the hand results in clawing.

The common peroneal nerve may be compressed between the lithotomy pole and the head of the fibula, resulting in foot drop.

The median nerve may be damaged by direct needle trauma or drug extravasation in the antecubital fossa. This results in paralysis of forearm pronators and weak wrist flexion. The thenar eminence muscles are paralysed, as are the flexors of the index and middle fingers. There is loss of sensation to the lateral half of the hand and the lateral 3½ fingers.

The radial nerve may be compressed as it winds around the spiral groove of the humerus. This results in wrist drop and a variable small area of anaesthesia over the root of the thumb.

The sciatic nerve (L4,5; S1,2,3) may be injured by poorly placed intramuscular injections in the gluteal region, resulting in foot drop and loss of sensation below the knee.

Q8.30

A = False
B = False
C = False
D = True
E = False

Positioning for neuraxial blockade may be difficult in this group of patients. Although spinal and epidural anaesthesia are associated with less blood loss and decreased deep venous thrombosis, this is not reflected in a longer-term decrease in out-of-hospital mortality compared to general anaesthesia at one month. A carefully managed anaesthetic using regional or general techniques, taking into account the patient's medical and physiological condition, is usually well tolerated. Up to 70% of patients having major hip surgery have some degree of deep venous thrombosis. Hypotensive anaesthesia decreases blood loss but is often contraindicated in the elderly, who have an increased incidence of cardiovascular and cerebrovascular disease.

Notes